LIFE OF THE MIND INTERRUPTED

LIFE OF THE MIND INTERRUPTED

ESSAYS ON MENTAL HEALTH AND DISABILITY IN HIGHER EDUCATION

KATIE ROSE GUEST PRYAL

Raven Books

Publisher's Cataloging-in-Publication Data

Pryal, Katie Rose Guest. 1976-.
Life of the Mind Interrupted: Essays on Mental Health and Disability in Higher Education / Katie Rose Guest Pryal
p.____ cm.____
ISBN 978-1-947834-05-7 (Pbk.) | 978-1-947834-06-4 (eBook)
1. Education, Higher. 2. Women College Teachers. 3. Autobiography. I. Title.
814'.54—dc23 | 2017952970

Raven Books

Published by Raven Books
an imprint of Blue Crow Publishing, LLC
Chapel Hill, NC
www.bluecrowpublishing.com
Cover Design by Lauren Faulkenberry

Katie Rose Guest Pryal is one of the foremost writers of disability and higher education we have today. Like Kay Redfield Jamison and Elyn Saks, Pryal pulls aside the curtain to look at what academic life is like for someone with a mental disability. With unmatched legal insight into the intersection of disability and university life, Pryal's writing is also accessible. Reading her writing is like sitting down to coffee with a friend. Covering vital topics such as disclosure, collegiality, and accommodations, *Life of the Mind Interrupted* helps academics and friends of academics navigate the thickets of higher education, where expectations of "sound mind" are cruelly at odds with the reality of disability. In Pryal's work we see hope: For a kinder, more just, more capacious understanding of what it means to be human, to pursue knowledge, and to educate.

— CATHERINE PRENDERGAST, PH.D.,
PROFESSOR OF DISABILITY STUDIES

CONTENTS

For my boys

INTRODUCTION

This is a book about mental illness and academia. But this is also a book about so much more than that: it's about grief, and friendship, and collegiality, and accessibility, and tragedy.

It is about trying to get by in a world that fears you, that believes you are unfit for your job, that wants to take your children away. A world whose police will kill you because you can't understand instructions.

The stakes for disabled people really are that high: life and death.

If you are a person with a disability, psychiatric or otherwise, and you've made it all the way to graduate school or to a job in the academy, then you have acquired quite a bit of privilege.

But we, psychiatrically disabled people in the academy, are reminded every day via news stories and personal stories shared by our friends, that our privilege can be stripped away by the groundless suspicions of our own colleagues, friends, and even family.

Our lives can be, in an instant, interrupted.

———

I was a junior in college when I finally realized that I was different in a way that my medically inclined parents would call "clinical." I'd always been a geeky kid, awkward at the parties my parents forced me to go to, only socializing, if at all, on a sports field. I was hard to be friends with, demanding, mercurial, with a terrible temper. I only had friends at all because I was also loyal, with big dreams. I loved hard. I also managed to find the weirdos who were like me.

But for the non-weirdos, I used words that were too long and too nerdy to ever be cool. *Who talks like that,* I remember one kid saying. Her words still bother me—because I also have trouble letting things go. I tried too hard in my classes in school, from middle school all the way through college. I checked out too many books from the library, and I never, ever said the right thing. It should surprise no one, therefore, that I became an academic.

For a while—meaning, during graduate school—things were great. I had friends who were all working hard toward similar goals, and we were achieving similar successes. Some of us dropped out to do other things that were cool—because we were now, among ourselves, unexpectedly cool in our individual, geeky ways. I'd also found a psychiatrist, and I had a diagnosis (bipolar disorder) and I listened to my doctor, and I had medicine that worked, and I took it like I was supposed to.

After twenty-five years or so, things seemed to be looking, for lack of a better word, normal.

———

But academia isn't an easy place to be if your brain isn't quite right. Contrary to what a lot of people think, there is no magic spark between mental illness and creativity. When I'm in a depressed funk, I can barely function. When I'm manic, I might have a lot of ideas, but they don't cohere, and later, when the mania subsides, trying to make sense of those manic ideas can be impossible.

Teaching, too, was hard. I taught a lot of courses at once, a lot of courses that I didn't feel any particular love for. I taught on a schedule that was terrible—first, I had the typical work load of an overworked graduate student, and then later, I had the typical work load of an overworked contingent faculty member. The teaching ground me down, like it does so many other contingent faculty: I taught a heavy, repetitive course load for little remuneration and experienced zero collegiality in my department.

After graduate school, I'd turned down good tenure-track jobs in favor of family and a city I love, and I don't regret it. After all, choosing to live with the person you love in a place that doesn't suck shouldn't mean, for me or for anyone, that my job must be unbearable. However, that's exactly what contingent academia means for many people, and that's what it meant for me. Studies have shown that giving employees more control over scheduling leads to a happier workforce,[1] yet I had no control over my schedule. And as psychologists Reevy and Deason's research showed, working in a contingent faculty position can literally be bad for a person's mental health.[2] It was certainly bad for mine.

I left my contingent faculty position back in 2014, and one of the very first things I did was write an article about keeping my psychiatric disability hidden from every institution I'd ever worked for. I'd spent over a decade in higher ed, and no one ever knew except for the select friends I'd chosen to disclose to because they were, indeed, my friends.

I'd spent my years in academia in hiding. Ironically, I'd worked as a disability studies scholar, yet I'd never discussed what it meant to live as a disabled person. So my first piece that I published tackled the issue of disclosure head-on. I called it "Disclosure Blues," and a wonderful editor at *Chronicle Vitae* at the time, Gabriela Montell, published it in June of 2014. And then, to my utter shock, she offered me a regular column on the subject of mental health, disability, and the academy, one that shares its title with this book, "Life of the Mind Interrupted." And I've been writing about mental health and disability ever since.

This book contains four sections. Part I, Disclosure Blues, introduces being psychiatrically disabled in the academy and the immediate challenges that a person might face. Part II, Collegiality, takes on the specific challenges that disabled people face when it comes to interacting with their colleagues in academia. Part III, Teaching, provides advice for how to make our teaching, for all of our students, disabled and normate alike, the most accessible and humane as it can be. And the last section, Part IV, "Beyond the Academy," tells three stories about my life as a disabled person outside of academia, because life doesn't stop at the doors of our departments and divisions. I hope that these essays can give both insight and hope to others who face similar challenges to mine.

———

A NOTE ON VOCABULARY

This book uses the preferred language of disabled activists, and, in particular, *this* disabled activist. Below is a list of terms with short explanations. Some of the terms you might know, but you might think they're the "wrong" terms. Some terms you might be unfamiliar with. That's okay.

Disabled person: I'm a disabled person. Most disabled people I know prefer this terminology to what has come to be known as "people-first language," which looks like this: "person with a disability." People-first language meant well, and it got us away from the dreaded terms like "a disabled," or "a schizophrenic," where the person was erased altogether. But there is nothing wrong with using the term "disabled" as an adjective.

Invisible disability: An invisible disability is a disability that isn't perceivable *as a disability* by others. For example, I talk very quickly, and sometimes blurt out the wrong thing. To outsiders, I might just seem over-caffeinated and awkward. I know that I have pressured speech, which is a symptom of my disability.

Neurodiversity: I'll use the dictionary definition on this one (OED): "the range of differences in individual brain function and behavioral traits, regarded as part of normal variation in the human population." Deriving from the word neurodiversity you get the adjective "neurodivergent." For example, I am neurodivergent.

Normate: Adjective or noun. A normate is a person who is not disabled. The term was coined by disability theorist Rosemarie Garland Thomson. A synonym that I use and that you might come across is "abled" or "able-bodied." I prefer "abled" to "able-bodied" because I often write about psychiatric disability, and "able-bodied" seems to emphasize physical disabilities. I prefer "normate" to all of them because of its simplicity.

Psychiatric disability: A psychiatric disability is a disability of the brain relating to mental illness. You can use "mental illness" as a synonym if you'd like. If you refer to people as "the mentally ill" that is Not Okay.

Spoons: This is one of my favorite words. "Spoons" is a disability community term used to describe and measure the energy it takes to perform daily tasks. The idea of "spoon theory" was created by Christine Miserandino in an essay, which you can download and read any time you'd like.[3] I recommend it.

September 2017

———

1. Erin L. Kelly, Phyllis Moen, and Eric Tranby, "Changing Workplaces to Reduce Work-Family Conflict: Schedule Control in a White-Collar Organization," *American Sociology Review*, April 2011, Volume 76, Issue 2, Pages 265–290. doi:10.1177/0003122411400056. The authors note, "Analyses clearly demonstrate that the workplace initiative positively affects the work-family interface, primarily by increasing employees' schedule control."

2. Gretchen M. Reevy and Grace Deason, "Predictors of Depression, Stress, and Anxiety Among Non-Tenure Track Faculty," *Frontiers in Psychology*, July 7, 2014, doi: 10.3389/fpsyg.2014.00701. Reevy and Deason point out the following negative outcomes for non-tenure-track faculty: "Specific demographic characteristics and coping strategies, inability to find a permanent faculty position, and commitment to one's organization predispose NTT faculty to perceive greater harm and more sources of stress in their workplaces. Demographic characteristics, lower income, inability to find a permanent faculty position, disengagement coping mechanisms (e.g., giving up, denial), and organizational commitment were associated with

the potential for negative outcomes, particularly depression, anxiety, and stress."

3. Christine Miserandino, "The Spoon Theory," *But You Don't Look Sick*, retrieved from butyoudontlooksick.com/articles/written-by-christine/the-spoon-theory/.

PART I
DISCLOSURE BLUES

DISCLOSURE BLUES

SHOULD YOU TELL COLLEAGUES ABOUT YOUR MENTAL ILLNESS?

A few years ago, I was thumbing through my latest teaching evaluations. At that point I'd been teaching university-level writing for many years, and reading teaching evaluations was nothing new. Mine were perennially strong, and I wasn't expecting anything different that semester.

But then I came across the single worst teaching evaluation I'd ever received. In retrospect, the student's tone resembled a toddler's temper tantrum. But at the moment I read it, the student's words struck in a very sensitive place, and they left me reeling. The student ended the evaluation with this pronouncement: "Prof. Pryal was often emotionally eratic" (misspelling and all).

In the pile of forty evaluations, only Mr. Eratic mentioned my alleged emotional misbehavior. But I felt stripped bare by the words. As a contingent (that is, non-tenure-track) professor, teaching evaluations were the near-exclusive criterion for my job retention. Most days at work, I felt what many academics who work off the tenure track feel: a persistent, low-grade anxiety about my lack of job security.

But I felt anxiety for another reason as well. I have a psychiatric disability—that is, a mental illness—that I've kept secret since I was diagnosed at the age of 21. So when the teaching evaluation called me "emotionally eratic," I feared that my supervisors would believe the words. And, despite all evidence to the contrary, I feared that Mr. Eratic might be right.

Mostly I feared that everyone at work would learn about my secret disability and that I would get fired because of it. I feared I would be seen as unreasonable and irrational, and therefore unable to do the work required of a professor. I feared that because of my disability, my career would be over.

Of course, my academic career didn't end with Mr. Eratic's course evaluation. I showed it to my boss, the director of my writing program, who pointed out the toddlerish tone and discounted the entire document with a chuckle. I chuckled too, nervously, and went on my way.

———

IT's BEEN years since that course evaluation, but I've never forgotten it. After I met with my boss, I tucked the evaluation away, along with my secret disability, for years—until I decided to take a leave of absence from teaching (back in 2014) and to start writing about mental health and academia in a more public way. I decided to start coming clean, so students like Mr. Eratic wouldn't be able to hurt me any more. (I'm lucky that my disability is invisible enough to allow me to pass as non-disabled. Not everyone has that privilege.)

Academia has had its share of mental-illness disclosure stories. Famously, there is that of Elyn Saks, a professor of law, psychology, and psychiatry and behavioral sciences at the University of Southern California. Saks, who has publicly discussed her schizophrenia in a 2007 memoir and a TED talk, knows about what it means to go public.

Saks points out the most obvious reason to disclose one's mental illness in the academic workplace—"the psychological benefits of not having a secret and being able to be open."[1] But she also writes about the many drawbacks of disclosure: "There is a tremendous stigma, still, around mental illness. People may believe, consciously or not, that you are unreliable or even dangerous, and they may fear you." Disclosure, she adds, may "have a big impact on your work life and your prospects for tenure."

Saks's advice is written from the position of a tenured professor with great academic privilege, the most important one being near-bulletproof job security. But there are other privileges that come with the type of job she holds. For example, she gives the following advice to professors with mental illness: "Schedule your courses carefully. If your meds make you tired in the morning, try not to teach morning classes. Try to choose courses that you like to teach—you will do a better job and feel less stressed." As any contingent professor knows, we often choose neither our courses nor our class meeting times. As a recent study by Reevy and Deason has showed, contingency is rarely good for your mental health.[2]

Lisa A. Tucker (formerly McElroy), a tenured professor of law at Drexel University, wrote for *Slate* in 2013 about her life as a professor with severe anxiety disorder.[3] Tucker began her academic career off the tenure track, in a stress-inducing, insecure job much like mine. Halfway through her teaching career—as the sole breadwinner for a family of four—she took a job on the tenure track. To her great relief, six years later, she earned tenure. She told me that she recognizes the incredible privilege tenure grants her: "You see, now that I have tenure, I am one of the very, very few people living with mental illness who does not have to worry about what might happen at work tomorrow," she explained. "I have a job for life."

I asked Tucker if she'd ever considered disclosing her disability prior to earning tenure. "Very few people in my life knew about my disability," she told me. "I was incredibly afraid of how I would be perceived if I told others. Before I got tenure, I just didn't feel safe."

But once she earned tenure, she felt a responsibility to speak on behalf of others who weren't so lucky: "Finally, I realized that many are truly prevented from disclosing because they don't have job security. Once I had tenure, I wasn't. I thought that I had a responsibility to speak out for those who couldn't." Tucker no longer worries that others will discover her disability —which is a big relief—but she still can "feel the panic in professional situations." After all, just because a person discloses her hidden disability, ableism in academia doesn't magically go away. She might no longer have the anxiety of keeping a secret, but now she must deal with the prejudices that her colleagues hold—consciously or no—against those with disabilities.

———

FOR EVERY SAKS OR TUCKER, though, there are many more academics who choose not to disclose their disabilities, especially psychiatric disabilities. I reached out to colleagues who have chosen to keep their invisible disabilities secret, asking them if they have any advice for others. They all expressed a strong fear of being discovered through my interviews of them, even despite my assurances that I would treat their words with the utmost privacy. Most of these folks are contingent professors.

One professor who teaches in a full-time contingent position at a top research university said she would only disclose her mental health issues "under subpoena." She believes that disclosing would hurt her job security because "contingent faculty can be so easily terminated." In her opinion, contingent —and even pre-tenure—professors simply don't have "the luxury to volunteer stigmatizing personal information."

"They hired you for your mind," she told me. "Why would you volunteer that there's something wrong with it?" She was quick to point out, though, that she doesn't "actually believe that a psychiatric disability necessarily means there is something wrong with your mind," just that other people can be "thoughtless."

One contingent humanities professor at another top research university noted that "some behaviors—such as obsessive-compulsive tendencies and social anxiety—are expected and even praised as the hallmarks of a serious thinker." She told me that she might even "joke about my 'neuroses' with colleagues with whom I am personal friends, but I will very rarely discuss (and certainly not in its entirety) treatment I have sought for these 'neuroses.'"

Furthermore, she never discusses more serious mental health issues, such as medication or depression, because of the stigma that tends to accompany them. Although this stigma is common everywhere, she told me, "in academia, one's brain is supposed to be the most essential asset one has."

Speaking with my colleagues, reading their words alongside McElroy's pre-tenure fears, remembering how anxious I felt reading the teaching evaluation that labeled me "emotionally eratic"—it's hard for me to suggest that graduate students, contingent faculty, or pre-tenure faculty disclose their psychiatric disabilities to their academic colleagues. We are, in academia, still devoted to the mythos of the good human speaking well, the professor as bastion of reason, the *cogito ergo sum*.

However, as McElroy told me, "every faculty is different." Reaching out in private to someone you trust to get a feel for the culture around you might help you make the best decision. And as Saks's and McElroy's stories—and my own—have shown, living out in the open has its benefits. Do your research. Figure out what feels safe to you, and act accordingly.

———

An earlier version of this chapter first appeared as a column in *Chronicle Vitae* on June 13, 2014.

1. Elyn R. Saks, "Mental Illness in Academe," *The Chronicle of Higher Education*, Nov. 25, 2009.
2. Gretchen M. Reevy and Grace Deason, "Predictors of Depression, Stress, and Anxiety Among Non-Tenure Track Faculty," *Frontiers in Psychology*, July 7, 2014, doi: 10.3389/fpsyg.2014.00701.
3. Lisa T. McElroy (now Tucker), "Worrying Enormously About Small Things," *Slate*, July 18, 2013.

SHE'S SO SCHIZOPHRENIC!

HOW NOT TO ALIENATE YOUR COLLEAGUES WITH PSYCHIATRIC DISABILITIES

Many people in the academy with invisible psychiatric disabilities—mental illnesses, that is—don't publicly disclose those disabilities. Like people in all walks of life, we often choose to stay quiet because we're afraid of the stigma attached to having a mental illness. But academics, in particular, often opt against disclosure because we work in a profession that is supposed to be the "life of the mind." If your mind doesn't work properly, how can you work properly?

That argument is counterfactual, of course, but that's how stigma works. It doesn't care about evidence.

Given how common psychiatric disabilities are, it's likely that we all know someone who has one. According to the National Alliance on Mental Illness and the National Institutes of Mental Health, between five and eight percent of adults have depression, three percent have bipolar disorder, and a whopping twenty percent have an anxiety disorder, such as obsessive-compulsive disorder or post-traumatic stress disorder.[1] Let's presume, for argument's sake, that similar numbers can be found in academia—even though some observers suggest that mental illness might be harder to treat or faster-growing in academia than in the average population.[2]

I'm aware of the criticisms, often flung by the antipsychiatry movement, that mental illness is over-diagnosed.[3] And I'm aware of arguments against the existence of mental illness at all. Disability studies is, after all, my field of research. But for the purpose of this article, I'm going to give our colleagues the benefit of the doubt and believe that their disabilities are real.

So if twenty-five to thirty percent of our colleagues likely have invisible psychiatric disabilities, and that they likely choose not to disclose, it's astounding how often members of the academy use objectively horrible language to describe our students and one another. I'm talking about language that uses specific psychiatric disabilities as insults—as though the disabilities themselves were insulting. We've all heard people use the r-word, and hopefully we understand why we shouldn't use that word to refer to people and things we just don't like.

Ableist language not only stigmatizes our colleagues with psychiatric disabilities, but it also teaches those without disabilities that using such language is OK.

In case you were wondering, using hurtful, ableist language is not OK.

Here's an example. Dr. Joseph P. Fisher, a university learning specialist, has worked throughout his career helping students with disabilities. One time he was working with a student earning a graduate degree in education. The student told him—in an offhand fashion, during a work session on a writing project—that her special-education professor kept using an acronym unfamiliar to her: "FLK." When the student asked the professor what "FLKs" were, the professor told her: "Funny Little Kids"—that is, kids with learning or developmental disabilities.

"The professor in question was being horrible about disabled children in front of a disabled adult with an invisible disability," Joseph told me. "Someone was saying this in an instructional setting at the graduate level."

Someone should have known better.

Here's how to avoid alienating your colleagues with psychiatric disabilities.

———

1. WATCH YOUR METAPHORS

"Bipolar," "autistic," "schizo," and "ADD" are words that we should never throw around casually in conversation. These words are descriptors of real psychiatric disabilities that people we know—people *you* know—actually possess. They are not metaphors for everyday behaviors that happen to bug us. When you use them to describe people you hate (by the way, why are we being so mean?), you imply that the disabilities themselves are something to be hated.

Martine (a pseudonym) is a full-time, non-tenure-track professor at a private university in the South who has an invisible psychiatric disability. She reported that, while she was in graduate school, she "regularly had people—other grad students and faculty—refer to my dissertation director as 'schizophrenic' because she was an energetic, yet very scattered, individual." Another faculty member in the department said to Martine: "No wonder it's taken you four years to finish your dissertation—your director is so schizophrenic!"

Martine explained that the faculty member making the insult meant "that it must be hard for me to stay on track with a director who was working on multiple projects and who had a hard time keeping to her own deadlines, much less keeping me to mine."

Martine's colleagues used the word "schizophrenic" as a metaphor for absent-minded, disorganized, and other qualities. In the case of Martine's advisor, no one actually believed the advisor suffered from schizophrenia. With their words, Martine's colleagues created a hostile environment for Martine, given Martine's own invisible psychiatric disability, and they revealed that they were ableist jerks.

They also revealed that they were really terrible at coming up with metaphors.

———

2. DON'T PLAY DOCTOR

You can buy the Diagnostic and Statistical Manual of Mental Disorders (DSM) at any bookstore and read all about the diagnostic criteria for psychiatric disabilities. With few exceptions—say, if you are actually studying psychology—please don't do this.

Some of the worst ableist-jerk insults aren't insults-by-metaphor, but the insults that arise when speakers think they know something about psychiatric disability. They diagnose, prescribe medications, and suggest therapeutic interventions, all from the faculty lounge. Unless you're a care provider, don't play at being one. At best, you mock the seriousness of your colleagues' disabilities and the real care they receive. At worst, you might cause actual harm if someone were to take your terrible advice.

Ava (a pseudonym) is a Latina, non-tenure-track professor at a small liberal arts college on the West Coast; she has an invisible psychiatric disability. She reports that colleagues often "complain about 'special snowflake' accommodations for students with mental health issues." Ava finds these complaints troubling and sometimes feels an urge to disclose her own disability to help explain "why these accommodations have nothing to do with the student being a snowflake and everything to do with them leading as normal a student life as possible."

Here's the problem: despite their complaints, Ava's colleagues simply do not know why these students with psychiatric disabilities need accommodations. After all, Ava's colleagues are not the students' doctors. These faculty presume that accommodations for invisible psychiatric disabilities must be fake, a pretense for cheating. To top it off, they voice these presumptions to Ava, their colleague with an invisible psychiatric disability—creating a hostile environment.

What is really mind-blowing is how the very same people

who will deny that one person has any kind of disability at all will turn around and say the opposite about someone else. Ava reports feeling uncomfortable when her colleagues declare that a person needs "to 'get on some meds' for whatever behavior s/he is having trouble dealing with."

"I'm sensitive to this," Ava explains, "because I'm aware my meds make it possible for me to function at the level I need to. But my meds work not because they're miracle drugs but because they've allowed me to listen to my illness through years of dialectic behavior therapy." Ava's colleagues' words—get on some meds—mock medication and how crucial it is to people with disabilities.

And when you know that someone actually has a disability, for the love of egg salad, do not use it against them. Never say, "Did you forget to take your meds today?" It's not your job to say something unless someone asked for your help.

Playing doctor all comes down to whether a disabled person is making the faculty member's life more difficult. Asking for accommodations? The disability is making the faculty member's life difficult, and so the disability must be fake. Acting in a way the faculty member doesn't like? There must be something wrong with you, so get on some meds to be more compliant and agreeable.

Playing doctor has nothing to do with the well-being of others. It has to do with being selfish.

Stop being selfish.

3. HOLD OTHERS ACCOUNTABLE

We should, when we can, hold others accountable for using hurtful, ableist language. Even gentle reminders—that we have better metaphors than "schizo," that playing at diagnosis is hurtful and selfish—can break down stigma and create a more welcoming environment for our colleagues.

When asked how she would react to a colleague using "bipolar" as an insult, Ava said: "As an ethnic minority, I don't spend a lot of energy policing people's language, or I'd never stop. But in that situation I'd probably say something along the lines of, 'X isn't bipolar—she's difficult,' adding some bit of humor." Ava is right: Humor breaks down defenses, making listeners more amenable to criticism. Often our colleagues don't realize that their comments are hurtful.

But sometimes you will encounter people whom you know you'll never change. This is the professor who uses the r-word to refer to freshmen who forget to bring their textbooks to class. This professor calls you the "PC Police" for pointing out ableist language. It's okay to write this professor off. It's okay to warn your friends about this professor, too. It's okay to never, ever let this professor know that you have a psychiatric disability— because it is likely that this professor will hold it against you.

Academia, like the rest of the world, has its share of irredeemable jerks. It's not our job to save them.

An earlier version of this chapter first appeared as a column in *Chronicle Vitae* on July 9, 2014.

1. National Alliance on Mental Illness, "Mental Illness by the Numbers" (not dated), retrieved from www.nami.org/Learn-More/Mental-Health-By-the-Numbers.

2. Claire Shaw and Lucy Ward, "Dark Thoughts: Why Mental Illness Is on the Rise in Academia," *The Guardian*, March 6, 2014.

3. Henry A. Nasrallah, MD, "The Antipsychiatry Movement: Who and Why," *Current Psychiatry*, Dec. 2011, Vol. 10, Issue 12, Pages 4-53.

SHATTERING THE MADNESS MONOLITH

ON THE INTERSECTIONS OF RACE, GENDER, AND PSYCHIATRIC DISABILITY

Working as an academic is hard enough without adding psychiatric disability to the mix. Academics worry about whether we should disclose their disabilities to colleagues. And we also must deal with the all-too-common ableist insults that some of these same colleagues toss around without a thought.

When we talk about psychiatric disability in the academy, we cannot ignore how race, gender, socioeconomic, and other kinds of privilege affect how people with disabilities live and work. It's a lot easier to deal with the stigma of mental illness if your colleagues aren't already questioning your competency on the job—overtly or not—because of which boxes you check on census forms.

Most of all, we must recognize that people with psychiatric disabilities do not experience their disabilities in a monolithic fashion. On the contrary, our diverse identities ensure that our experiences of disability are also diverse. For example, the National Alliance on Mental Illness has designated July as Minority Mental Health Month to draw attention to the dramatic differences in how mental health is addressed across various racial and ethnic communities in the United States, including (and perhaps especially) by mental health professionals.

Race and other types of privilege can affect how we experience psychiatric disability in the academy. Dominic (a pseudonym) is a white, straight, male, tenure-track faculty member at a public regional university. He has an anxiety disorder. He reports that he doesn't hear many ableist insults, even though, he tells me, "Academics can be such terrible human beings. It really is astounding." He believes that his colleagues avoid using hurtful language around him because he is "out" with his disability in his department and because of his "enormous privileges." He describes how his social position plays an important role in how he is treated: "I have a pretty good presence, am white, male, tenure-track, extremely verbal, and I disclose my anxiety and panic disorders without a trace of apology (because I've been doing so for some time). In these circumstances, even crappy people typically don't feel comfortable saying much of anything in my presence."

Dominic recognizes that, while all who are psychiatrically disabled are subject to stigma, privilege can make stigma easier to bear. Because of his race, gender, sexuality, and job status, his colleagues afford him a presumption of competence. The presumption affects how his colleagues treat him, and how he expects to be treated.

All people with psychiatric disabilities are familiar with the presumption of incompetence attached to having what others perceive to be a broken brain. Add to this presumption the myriad others—for example, that women are bad at math, that black women scientists can be abused with impunity, that female academics who are mothers aren't worthy of the tenure track (not that there's much of a tenure track left)—and often you end up with the makings of an academic train wreck.

But not always. Here are three stories of academic women of color with psychiatric disabilities. These stories show, in three unique ways, how the presumption of incompetence can lead scholars down unexpected paths. But each woman has found her successes, too.

CARA: "MY LIFE IS RUN BY MY CONDITIONS"

Cara (a pseudonym) is a female, queer, African-American doctoral student in pharmacology. She has a physical disability (lupus) and a psychiatric disability (bipolar disorder). When I spoke with her, she was in the final months of her Ph.D. program. She told me, "I don't think the intersectionality of my mental illness and personal identity have affected my work in an identifiable way." However: "Having a mental illness and physical illness while trying to complete a challenging course of study like pharmacology is an awesome feat that is extremely isolating sometimes."

This February, Cara's lupus caused her to have a stroke,

which took three weeks to recover from. "Often I feel as if my life is run by my conditions," she tells me. "I'm always running from one appointment to the next." Her disability sometimes keeps her from participating in departmental life: "I often give in to my social anxiety and avoid events because I feel so out of place—not because of my gender, race, or sexuality, but because of my disability."

Cara was also forced to change her course of study due to her disability. First, she had to switch from medical school to her doctoral program. Then, rather than accommodate her and let her keep her research plan, the university pushed her into changing paths: "In part because of my recurrent depression and physical limitations, I had to change labs, from bench work with cells to translational-clinical work with humans." She's still unhappy about this "soft forced choice": "There are low points and high points like any research project, but they are tinged by a sense of resentment."

But finishing a doctorate in Pharmacology is an "awesome feat" indeed.

———

ANNIE: "MAYBE THEY JUST REALLY LOVE T'AI CHI"

Annie (a pseudonym) is a Chinese-American, straight, female university professor. While she was in graduate school, she found it difficult to receive medical treatment due to the perceived psychiatric condition of simply being Asian and female: "I went to a doctor at the university because I had recurring abdominal pain. The doctor listened to my description, but rather than doing a physical exam, he explained to me that it was normal for Asian women to be anxious and stressed out, and anxiety was probably causing my abdominal pain." But surprisingly, the doctor didn't treat the anxiety either. He just said there was nothing he could do.

Annie was persistent, though, and another doctor diagnosed her with a medical problem unrelated to anxiety and treated her successfully. Annie remains struck, however, by the first doctor's reaction to her race and gender: "Having a doctor declare a mental issue to be 'normal' because of my race has stuck with me through the years."

Annie's terrible experience with the university doctor is doubly complicated. First, he failed to diagnose a real gastrointestinal illness because of a psychiatric illness he'd imagined solely because of Annie's race. Second, he refused to treat the imaginary psychiatric illness, declaring it a facet of being an Asian woman—and therefore untreatable. Annie's doctor diagnosed her with a psychiatric illness and then deliberately did not treat the illness because of her race.

The problem, according to Annie (and to the American Psychological Association), is that Asian-American women are at high risk of suicide—higher than Asian-American men. Furthermore, Asian Americans often don't seek mental health care for cultural reasons, such as fear of shaming their families or lack of trust in traditional (white) mental-health-care systems. Comedian Kristina Wong describes how she had trouble identifying with "psychology brochures featuring stock images of white women looking forlorn against rain-specked windows."

Wong writes, with fake incredulity: "Chinese people didn't see therapists. Spend $100 to tell a stranger your problems?" Annie's experience only reinforced the idea that Asian Americans shouldn't trust white doctors.

At the end of our interview, Annie asked me a question that seemed out of the blue: "Do doctors ever tell you that you should try T'ai Chi?"

I am a white, straight woman. "No," I laughed. "Never."

Annie told me, "I have had no fewer than five non-Asian doctors—psychiatrists and medical doctors—tell me that I should try T'ai Chi as a treatment for my illnesses. Maybe it's because of my race." She paused. "Or maybe they just really love T'ai Chi."

—————

RUTH: "THE EXPECTATION IS THAT I GRIN AND BEAR IT"

Ruth C. White, a decorated professor of social work at the University of Southern California, is an immigrant Black woman who identifies with the queer community. Despite her many professional successes, she points to various facets of her identity, including being a Black woman, that have put her credentials as an academic into question: "Being a mother, I have found that my 'competence' is an issue that hangs in the air but remains unspoken. As a Black woman, the expectation is that I grin and bear it."

Back when she was on her job search, she did not want anyone to know about her psychiatric disability, bipolar disorder: "I have had concerns when job hunting, that it's bad enough being a Black woman, but being a 'crazy' one may be a deal-breaker." Ruth shared her disability with her colleagues and more publicly around the time she published her first book, *Bipolar 101: A Practical Guide to Identifying Triggers, Managing Medications, Coping with Symptoms, and More.* Since then she has published widely on the intersection of mental illness and race.

Ruth worried not only about how her colleagues would view her disability, but also about how her students would view it: "I used to be concerned about how students would view me and my 'competence' if they knew I was mentally ill." But, she explains, since her students have learned of her disability, her experience "has only been very positive." Indeed, she has become a beacon for her students: "Students with mental illness (and without) see me as a role model and feel safe to come to me when they are having a hard time or seeking guidance and support."

Now that she's a professor in a major school of social work, Ruth feels a sense of responsibility toward her profession: "Being in a position to shape professional minds regarding the topic and experience of mental illness, I feel obligated to give them insight beyond 'abnormal psychology.' I know that not all mentally ill people can be university professors, but I also want them to know what it's like to live with a chronic, severe mental illness and thrive."

Ruth lives a successful professional life. She wants the experts in her field to know that others with mental illness can do the same.

_____

MONOLITHS SHATTERED

The stories of Dominic, Cara, Annie, and Ruth reveal the diverse ways that people live with psychiatric disability in the academic workplace. With the presumption of incompetence following you around, every academic with a psychiatric disability knows what it is like to have to work extra hard to prove that you can do your job.

But our experiences of disability are not monolithic across race, gender, and sexuality, as these stories show. We shouldn't presume everyone's story is the same as our own.

We should all take time to listen.

_____

An earlier version of this chapter first appeared as a column in _Chronicle Vitae_ on July 31, 2014.

BREAKING THE MAD GENIUS MYTH

I can't believe it's been more than 20 years since the suicide of Kurt Cobain, the charismatic front man of Nirvana. Images of his 27-year-old face—those piercing blue eyes, his stringy, blond, chin-length hair, framing the sharp contours of his unshaven face—seem ubiquitous around every anniversary of his death. HBO produced a 2015 documentary, *Kurt Cobain: Montage of Heck*, and with it followed innumerable features in both print and online magazines (not least of which, the cover story in the April 23, 2015, issue of *Rolling Stone*), all of which made me feel wistful and heartbroken all over again. Every image and story about Cobain and his death catapulted me back to one magical November night during my senior year in high school, when my girlfriends and I risked serious punishment by staying out well past curfew to see Nirvana on their "In Utero" tour.

It was well worth it: We had the rare opportunity to see them in a small venue, the Armory in Philadelphia, and be among 3,000 members of our grunge generation. It would be the last time we'd see them. A few short months later, Cobain would be dead.

Like so many others, I was shocked when I heard about his suicide—I was listening to the radio when the news broke regular programming. I was shocked not only because of the news itself, but because he wasn't much older than me, and his death felt all too real and uncomfortably accessible. I had just seen him, up close. He'd been singing to me, my friends, and a few-thousand other kids of our generation, not that long ago—and now he was ... dead? I was 17 at the time, trying to wrap my mind around it. Kurt Cobain was the first famous person to whom I related who had done something so tragic. He had *committed suicide.*

My friends and I struggled to make sense of this unthinkable act. If Kurt Cobain could end it all, when he had a wife and new baby, when he seemed to have the perfect life, we needed to figure out the logic of his violent act.

And we came up with a logic, if a misguided one: We had decided that it was his genius that killed him. That being so brilliant and talented was too much to bear.

We were wrong, but hey, we were young.

Now, you can debate whether Cobain was a genius, but there is little doubt that he changed the entire landscape of popular music in the early 1990s. As Sarah Larson wrote in *The New Yorker,* "My generation talks about hearing *Nevermind* for the first time, and seeing 'Smells Like Teen Spirit' on MTV, the way our parents talk about seeing the Beatles on *The Ed Sullivan Show.*"[1]

There was something romantic to our young, naïve minds about the idea of a tormented, suicidal genius: it's tragic; it's even beautiful. Our belief in death-by-genius allowed my friends and I to say good-bye to our hero with respect.

There is a problem with the suicidal genius, the tormented artist, and all such similar stereotypes—they are a sleight-of-hand, a sideshow, and not respectful of the dead, or the living, at all.

———

EVERY TIME A FAMOUS ACTOR, writer, or other artist commits suicide, arguments come pouring in about the supposed connections between creativity, genius, and the tormented artist. The recent suicides of Robin Williams, Chris Cornell, and others keep bringing these supposed connections to the fore.

But how does the stereotype of the "mad genius" affect actual people living with psychiatric disabilities?

Psychiatrist Nancy C. Andreasen, who claims "dual identities as a scientist and a literary scholar," is one of three leading scientists interested in drawing connections between mental illness and creative genius (along with Arnold Ludwig and Kay Redfield Jamison). In a feature for *The Atlantic*, Andreasen reported on her ongoing work searching for the "Secrets of the Creative Brain."[2] She wrote about how she analyzed cutting-edge MRI scans of creative people's brains, looking for, as she puts it, "a little genie that doesn't exist inside other people's heads."

Some scientists, and a few journalists, speak against this "mad genius" research. Psychology researcher Arne Dietrich, in *Frontiers in Psychology*, took a stand against what he called "The Mythconception of the Mad Genius."[3] Dietrich ran the numbers, and in doing so he made a strong case opposing the mad genius myth: "It isn't my goal here to make a case for the opposite claim, but, by all evidence, it is hard to escape that conclusion. By the looks of these numbers, I would wager good money that the link between mental illness and genius is negative. To be exact: extremely negative." On a similar note, Scott Barry Kaufman, a trained psychologist, who works as a science writer, wrote for the *Scientific American* blog about "The Real Link Between Creativity and Mental Illness."[4] He led off his piece with this bold statement: "[L]et me nip this in the bud: Mental illness is neither necessary nor sufficient for creativity."

In my research, I can find surprisingly few who will speak against the mad genius myth despite a lack of strong scientific evidence to support it. Andreasen got a prominent feature in a prominent magazine, which gives her research a halo of respectability. It is as though we, as a society—just like me and my teenaged friends—want to believe the myth is true.

The mad genius myth is essentially a Romantic stereotype. And that's big-R "Romantic." For example, as evidence of creative genius, Andreasen recounts an old tale wherein Samuel Taylor Coleridge composed his epic poem Kubla Khan "while in an opiate-induced, dreamlike state, and began writing it down when he awoke." But, alas, he "lost most of it when he got interrupted and called away on an errand." Errands, it seems, are not romantic.

————

Andreasen's work, and similar work by others, gets a lot of airplay because we as a society are fascinated by the notion of the mad genius. But this fascination has negative consequences for people with psychiatric disabilities. The issue here is whether the mad genius stereotype—the stereotype that psychiatric disability and creativity are somehow linked—gets in the way of saving people's lives or making their lives more livable.

And there is real evidence that it does.

The mad genius stereotype limits how people with psychiatric disabilities are allowed to exist in the world. As psychologist Judith Schlesinger notes, focusing on the mad genius treats people with "exceptional gifts" as psychologically abnormal.[5] If you are a genius with a mental illness, then you are at risk of being pathologized by doctors eager to scan your brain looking for Andreasen's "little genies."

And if you have a psychiatric disability and you are *not* a creative genius, then all you have left is a broken brain—right? You have nothing positive to redeem your disability.

Either way, research and clinical experience shows that the mad genius stereotype affects how people with disabilities seek and receive treatment, whether we work in creative fields or not.

For example, the mad genius stereotype hurts because it creates yet another stereotype that people with psychiatric disabilities have to fight against—and we have enough of those. We already have to deal with various kinds of stigma—the stigma of irrationality, for example, and the stigma of dangerousness. Because of stigma, those of us with invisible disabilities often opt to pass as non-disabled to avoid being mistreated by neurotypical (i.e., non-disabled) colleagues, friends, and family.

The mad-genius stereotype creates even more stigma.

Here's an example. Say you work in a field that prizes calmness, rationality, reason, and predictability—qualities that are opposite of those possessed by the stereotypical mad genius. Say you are a lawyer, say you are really smart about the law—a law professor, like I was for many years. When I was working at a law school, I was terrified that anyone I worked with would find out about my mental illness, as I talked about in Chapter 1 of this book.

Why wouldn't I be afraid? After all, the mad genius myth encourages people to believe that people with mental illness are mercurial and unpredictable. Think about it: they put their heads in ovens (like Sylvia Plath), walk into rivers (like Virginia Woolf), and cut off their ears (like Vincent van Gogh).

I always feared that if my law school colleagues were to discover my psychiatric disability, I would lose my job—maybe not directly (that would be illegal, probably) but, you know, indirectly. Promotion and retention in academia come down to secretive votes. Your colleagues rarely must provide reasons for why they choose to vote the way they do.

And given the stereotype of the mad genius, my colleagues, those who would vote on my promotion and retention, might have believed that I was unfit for my job as a law professor. They might have believed that, because of the mad genius stereotype, I could therefore not be lawyerly; I could not possibly be calm, rational, reasonable, or predictable. Never mind that recent studies show that law students and lawyers have some of the highest rates of mental illness of any population in the United States—approaching forty percent according to the nonprofit David Nee Foundation.[6]

I feared for my job, and the stigma created by the mad genius stereotype was part of the reason why.

———

THE MAD GENIUS stereotype attacks from two angles: few people can live up to the immense psycho-biographies attributed to geniuses like Sylvia Plath or David Foster Wallace. The expectations those writers, artists, composers and the like set are way too high for the most ordinary humans to meet.

And no law professor can provide enough reassurance to her dean that she is *not* a "mad" genius, when her dean is secretly afraid that she will deliver her lectures in Coleridgean dream-like states.

But the mad genius stereotype affects more than just the way that neurotypical people view people with psychiatric disabilities. It affects how people with psychiatric disabilities view ourselves and the decisions we make about our treatment.

For example, as a way of battling self-stigma, people with psychiatric disabilities sometimes deliberately request certain diagnoses from their doctors. In particular, in recent years, patients have requested the diagnosis of bipolar disorder. Patients associate this diagnosis with, among other positive attributes, being creative. Indeed, psychiatric researchers Diana Chan and Lester Sireling observed that "self-diagnosis of bipolar disorder" reflects the patient's "aspirations for higher social status, as illustrated by the implicit association of bipolar disorder with celebrity status and creativity."[7] In short, patients want to be bipolar because news coverage of the mad genius stereotype depicts bipolar disorder as cool.

For the record, bipolar disorder is not "cool." It is what it is: a disability that is mine—and many others'—and we don't deserve to be persecuted for it. But romanticizing a disability, any disability, is ableist.

Furthermore, romanticizing bipolar disorder is *dangerous*. Chan and Sireling point out how important getting the correct diagnosis is for the health of a patient: "Often unknown to patients who 'want to be bipolar' are the consequences of being diagnosed with the disorder. These range from less burdensome psychosocial issues such as obligatory declarations of mental illness to employers and medical insurance companies, to the medical risks of potential treatment with teratogenic mood stabilizers, genetic predisposition to other mental illness and a potentially increased risk of suicide." At the same time, they note, "[I]t could be considered equally harmful, if not more so, to miss a true bipolar diagnosis."

———

I TALKED about this kind of "diagnosis shopping" with Dr.

Kenan Penaskovic of the Department of Psychiatry at the University of North Carolina School of Medicine. Dr. Penaskovic has found in his practice that "some patients gravitate toward illnesses that may be perceived as more socially acceptable or that carry better prognoses." Bipolar disorder is certainly one of those "better" illnesses. Schizophrenia and borderline personality disorder are examples of illnesses that patients gravitate away from, he notes. Patients with schizophrenia and borderline "may strongly prefer to be classified as bipolar" both because bipolar disorder has "a better prognosis" and because it is "more socially acceptable" than either schizophrenia or borderline personality disorder.

But why is bipolar disorder becoming more socially acceptable? Dr. Penaskovic recognizes that it is "in part due to celebrities." And although he is glad that the stigma against bipolar disorder seems to be lessening, he notes that "it is important to remember that most individuals with bipolar disorder are not extraordinarily creative." Rather, they "more commonly suffer from devastating depression and debilitating manic episodes."

The fact that bipolar disorder tends to be a disease with terrible symptoms has not stopped the rise in its diagnosis. Dr. Penaskovic pointed out that the editors of the DSM-5, the latest edition of the Diagnostic and Statistical Manual of Mental Disorders put out by the American Psychiatric Association (released in 2013), "recognized bipolar was being more commonly—and potentially overly—diagnosed," and the editors have altered the diagnostic criteria to account for this rise in diagnoses.

———

In addition to causing diagnosis shopping, the mad-genius stereotype also affects how patients respond to their doctors or make decisions about their treatment. Researchers find that patients are citing the mad genius stereotype as a reason for refusing to take their medications and for ceasing all treatment for their psychiatric disabilities. Doctors report that their patients believe—without evidence—that their treatments will cause them to lose creativity.

According to Andreasen and her co-author Glick, there is ample scientific evidence, however, that treatment will prevent psychosis, depression, and death without affecting creative output at all.[8] Two of the leading researchers who have put forward the link between mental illness and creativity—Dr. Andreasen and Dr. Kay Redfield Jamison—both support the treatment of psychiatric disabilities. These are two of the three doctors who helped create the mad genius stereotype as we know it today, and yet they both support treatment. Dr. Andreasen co-authored an article on bipolar disorder and creativity in which she concluded, "In general, creative individuals are most productive when their affective symptoms are under good control." And, as Dr. Jamison observed in a report on her mad-genius research for *Scientific American*, "No one is creative when severely depressed, psychotic or dead."[9]

———

But these are the words of doctors and researchers. We, as

disabled people, get to have our say about our care, and our symptoms, and our creativity. And much, indeed, has been said. Since Jamison, Andreasen, and the rest have put forward the mad genius myth, so much has been written that there is arguably a full-blown treatment-versus-creativity debate.

Journalist and essayist Gila Lyons asked rhetorically, in the literary magazine *The Millions*, "What if the touch of the madness had been medicated out of van Gogh, Hemingway, Fitzgerald, Faulkner, Sexton, Plath, and [David Foster] Wallace?"[10] Her words imply belief in the mad genius stereotype, which holds that, first, creativity is necessarily tied to madness, and, second, that creativity is a thing that would be "medicated out" of a person. In her essay, Lyons debated whether she herself should take psychiatric medication. She describes in devastating detail how she suffered with anxiety and panic disorders, and finally settled on psychiatric treatment despite a fear that she would stop writing. And, she describes, she did stop writing—or, rather, she stopped writing the way she used to: "I used to write to live, to push myself out of a dark hole and connect with a reader in the world outside my suffocating den. Now, though I don't feel quite as alive when I'm not writing, it's no longer imperative." Writing before she treated her psychiatric disability was, it seems, a kind of treatment itself. Now, she writes, "Though it takes more discipline to sit down and write now, since I am not doing so to save my life, I am practicing writing from a place of curiosity rather than pain, fascination rather than desperation, forging my way more safely into a different dark." We must respect the truth Lyons's experience—her writing practice changed once she no longer had untreated anxiety and panic disorders.

But the question I struggle with, the problem I have with the mad genius myth—a myth I, too, bought into in my twenties, to my own detriment—is this: If there were no mad genius myth, would Lyons, would I, would others like us have struggled so long to seek treatment? How much extra suffering does the mad genius myth create? The modern-day creators of the myth themselves (Andreasen, Jamison) are strong proponents of adequate treatment—yet the myth creates fear in those of us who do creative work—needless fear. Why? The myth has such a strong hold in the popular consciousness while its mortal reality—that the vast majority of people with psychiatric disorders do not do creative work, that the vast majority of creative people do not have severe psychiatric disorders, that proper treatment does not (or need not) have the side effect of screwing up your creative abilities (or your libido, or your body weight et cetera).

In direct response to Lyons's piece, writer, singer, and songwriter Tasha Golden wrote for the blog of the literary magazine *Ploughshares* that "the fear of control feeds the myth that creativity is some kind of Mysterious, Mad Magic. It's not."[11] Golden points out that an over-reliance on "Magical-Muse thinking" actually disempowers creative workers. She suggests setting aside belief in such thinking to "empower ourselves and each other to make more and better work. And to be healthy while we're at it." The difference, according to Golden, lies in discipline. She urges us all to "stop seeing intention as inferior to 'inspiration.'" She writes of "sober intention, healthful presence, and the humility of artistic responsibility." She argues that we should stop allowing mental illness to rob us of responsibility by believing that it either provides a person with inspiration that day *or not*. That is, indeed, disempowering thinking. As artistic workers, we are responsible for our own artist output.

But what rang most true to me was this: The notion that a person should deliberately not treat a disability in order to suffer in order to create—is, when I think about it, incredibly ableist. What *if* Chris Cornell had been treated, or David Foster Wallace, or Kurt Cobain? I sure wish Cobain were alive to see his baby girl grow up. His death was a tragedy, period. He only released three studio albums. How many more did he have in him? (For comparison, Springsteen was already on number seven when he released *Born in the USA*.)

Worse, these deaths were perhaps avoidable if we lived in a society that provided adequate mental health care and did not stigmatize or romanticize mental illness.

———

Lyons's and Golden's words reveal in a public fashion the struggle that many patients have faced privately. Because of the mad genius stereotype, patients in creative fields (and even those who aren't) make treatment decisions that they believe will make them more creative. These decisions often come at the detriment of their health, as Nancy Andreasen herself has observed. In particular, for patients with bipolar disorder, Andreasen has noted, "Some feel that the high energy levels and euphoria associated with manic or hypomanic states enhance creativity"—and her patients are afraid to lose that perceived enhanced creativity.[12] When I was first diagnosed with bipolar disorder in my early twenties, I was lured into this kind of thinking. A few years of misery later, I changed my mind.

In response to this belief, and perpetuated by the mad-genius stereotype, patients—including a younger me—often choose to forego psychiatric treatment, both medication and therapy. But, as Andreasen's and others' research has shown, scaling back medication is usually the wrong course of treatment, even for creative people with bipolar disorder. Andreasen advocates instead for a normal course of treatment for bipolar patients, observing "it is likely that reducing severe manic episodes may actually enhance creativity in many individuals." This has been my own experience.

And, as Tasha Golden writes in her experience as a disabled person: "I've written far more post-depression than I ever did before."

———

An earlier version of this chapter first appeared as an essay in *DAME Magazine* on April 22, 2015.

1. Sarah Larson, "Impact, Influence, and Awesomeness: Nirvana Redeems the Rock and Roll Hall of Fame Ceremony," *The New Yorker*, April 14, 2014.

2. Nancy C. Andreasen, "Secrets of the Creative Brain," *The Atlantic*, July 2014.

3. Arne Dietrich, "The Mythconception of the Mad Genius," *Frontiers in Psychology*, Feb. 26, 2014, DOI:10.3389/fpsyg.2014.00079.

4. Scott Barry Kaufman, "The Real Link Between Creativity and Mental Illness," *Scientific American*, Oct. 3, 2013.

5. Judith Schlesinger, "Creative Mythconceptions: A Closer Look at the Evidence for the "Mad Genius" Hypothesis," *Psychology of Aesthetics, Creativity, and the Arts*, 2009, Volume 3, Issue 2, Pages 62-72. DOI:10.1037/a0013975.

6. Dave Nee Foundation, "Lawyers and Depression" (no date), retrieved from http://www.daveneefoundation.org/scholarship/lawyers-and-depression/.

7. Diana Chan and Lester Sireling, "'I want to be bipolar' . . . A New Phenomenon," *The Psychiatrist*, 2010, Volume 34, Pages 103-105. DOI:10.1192/pb.bp.108.022129.

8. Nancy C. Andreasen and Ira D. Glick, "Bipolar Affective Disorder and Creativity: Implications and Clinical Management," *Comprehensive Psychiatry*, 1988, Volume 29, Issue 3, Pages 207-217.

9. Kay Redfield Jamison, "Manic-Depressive Illness and Creativity," *Scientific American*, Feb. 1995, Pages 44-49.

10. Gila Lyons, "Creativity and Madness: On Writing Through the Drugs," *The Millions*, Feb. 27, 2014.

11. Tasha Golden, "Creativity Is Neither Magic Nor Madness," *The Ploughshares Round-Down*, March 2014.

12. Nancy C. Andreasen, "The Relationship Between Creativity and Mood Disorders," *Dialogues in Clinical Neuroscience*, 2008, Volume 10, Issue 2, Page 251.

WORKING WHEN YOUR BRAIN ISN'T

E verything is terrible.
       Everything isn't terrible. My kids are off to school.
The mortgage is paid, and it will continue to be paid for the
foreseeable future. We have food, and we have clothing.
Abraham Maslow would say we're fine. Abraham Maslow
would say things are not terrible. Abraham Maslow would say I
need some perspective.

My husband says: Sometimes life is just hard. And that's
true. But sometimes, hard things are harder for some people
than for others. Sometimes, everything is terrible and you can't
see things any other way.

And yesterday I just discovered that my child's after-school
program may be neglecting him and leaving him to be bullied by
older kids. I'm going to have to go confront the director and
probably pull my son from the program. Pulling him will
require me to completely reorganize my schedule because my
workday will end at 2:30 p.m., instead of at 5:30 p.m.

All of that would be easier, however, if getting out of bed didn't feel like the equivalent of hauling a boulder across the Bonneville Salt Flats, barehanded and barefoot.

My husband will not have to reorganize his work life. I'm trying to not think about that though, because thinking about how my husband will not have to reorganize his work life will only make me feel like things are more terrible.

Things are terrible because my body feels like a brick and I can't move.

The thought of confronting the woman who runs the after-school program makes me want to die. I don't like confronting people, although my husband tells me that I'm good at it. Confrontations are draining and leave me feeling shaky and lost for the rest of the day.

I feel shaky and lost all of the time right now.

I just scheduled a meeting with the director of the after-school program for two days from now. I will arrive with a dossier of notes, an agenda, and I will succeed. Because that is what I do.

I succeed, even when I feel shaky and lost.

I blame myself for not noticing that my child was unhappy at the after-school program. He is sweet and sensitive. He told me yesterday that he felt afraid to tell me he was unhappy. He's never felt afraid to tell me things before. I ask myself: Why now? What have I done? It must be my fault.

Except rationally, I know it isn't my fault. I can see where the fault lies. That's why I will succeed. Even though I feel shaky and lost.

Everything is terrible because food doesn't taste right.

Nothing in our refrigerator is appealing—even the takeout my husband ordered last night from the amazing Italian restaurant in our neighborhood that puts bacon in everything. How can vodka sauce covered in bacon not taste good? When vodka sauce covered in bacon doesn't taste good you know everything is terrible.

Right now I'm supposed to be writing—and you are supposed to be reading—about living the life of the mind with a mental illness. I'm supposed to be writing—and you are supposed to be reading—about how to work in and around academia with a psychiatric disability. Right now you might be thinking: Why am I reading this meandering mess?

Everything is so terrible that my brain just isn't working. How can you live the life of the mind when your brain isn't working? This is the terrible secret that a person living the life of the mind with a psychiatric disability never wants to share.

My brain. It isn't working.

Yet sometimes, some weeks, this brain comes up with so many ideas I have to use the voice recorder on my cell phone to capture them into emails I can send to myself. I have tons of notes full of ideas. I have so many ideas I have spreadsheets to sort them, to classify them, to rate them, and to date them.

But right now, I look at these ideas and they seem like they were written by another person.

A person who is alive.

Right now I can barely keep my eyes open to stare at my computer screen. It is 10:30 in the morning. I think: I should probably have more coffee. I think: More coffee will help me.

But caffeine with its tainted energy doesn't fix depression. It just makes you more aware of how depressed you are.

I think: Maybe I'll watch a movie. The more ridiculous the movie is, the better. I'll escape into a movie and then I won't have to think about my suffering child and losing 15 hours a week of my workday (and how my husband will not be sharing that burden with me) and how my books aren't selling as well as I'd hoped and how everything I touch seems to rot rot rot. Captain America would be a good choice. He's a peppy dude.

Except as I watch the movie all I can think about is how I should be working instead. I have no fewer than three books to write at the moment. Then I look at the piles of laundry that haven't been washed in over two weeks—because if I don't do it, who will? So I drag myself to the laundry room to run a load, and the pile of laundry seems to grow even as I stare at it. And how is that even possible? I'm going to be washing five or six loads easy. Who is going to fold all of this? And when?

Why wasn't I born a man? Why isn't there any good child care? Why don't we have gun control? Why aren't my books selling? Why can't I finish my latest manuscript? Why can't I enjoy a movie with Scarlett Johansson in a black bodysuit and Chris Evans in a blue one?

I don't ask, "What is the matter with me?" because I already know the answer to that question.

I never write when I'm depressed because it's too hard. Nothing makes any sense. Sentences aren't sentences and parts of speech don't fall into the right places.

What would an editor do with a written manifestation of

depression, I think. And that is the first thought today that has made me smile.

————

TWO YEARS LATER

When I wrote this original column two years ago, I was in a depressed state—not as bad as the depressed states I'd experienced before I was diagnosed with bipolar disorder and before I started treatment, but still pretty bad. Depression for me, now—for the most part—doesn't dip as low and doesn't last as long as before I started treatment. But when I do grow depressed, one of the most difficult aspects to deal with is how I lose the ability to simply *make words*. When I don't have words, I can't ask for help. I can't answer questions. I can't form memories.

I don't have any of the tools I need to make sense of the world.

When I first wrote this column I knew, because I'm very aware of my moods now, that I was depressed. And I knew, because I'm aware of what happens when I'm depressed, that I would forget most of what happened that day, that week, maybe even that month. So I started writing, even though I knew the words wouldn't make sense.

And I was right: the sentences didn't make sense. Most of the sentences ended up as fragments and most of those fragments ended with question marks. The question-fragments were non-sequiturs, and I didn't care, I just wanted to get the jumble recorded because, even though depression for me is not rare, a recording of it was.

I also knew that research shows that people who experience depression often suffer from memory loss. When you're depressed, growth of brain cells in your hippocampus (the area of your brain that helps make memories) is suppressed. Memory loss like I experienced is likely biologically based.[1]

And I figured that others who experience depression might benefit from hearing from someone else who is like them and who is trying to figure out an ordinary day while sick. And I figured that those who don't know what depression is like might benefit from being immersed in the closest thing I could provide to a depression amusement-park ride: a play-by-play description of a day in my life. But the thing was, there was no way to recreate that play-by-play after the fact. It had to happen in the moment. So that's what I did. I sat down and wrote the jumble. And then the next day, I revised it a bit, turning the question-fragments into sentences. And then next day, I emailed that batch of sentences to my editor at the magazine, and she published it.

But I realize, now, that no matter how hard I try to explain what it means to try to go about a day when sick, depressed, *disabled*, I'll never be able to adequately do so. The arrow will never strike true. You either know what it's like, or you don't know. And that thought, that outsiders will never really know, scares me. Because it means that forever I will be, on some level, at the mercy of strangers and whether they possess the ability to imagine a life that is different than their own. At the mercy of editors who are willing to publish strange pieces that may not make complete sense. At the mercy of bosses or clients who are understanding. At the mercy of family and friends who cut me slack.

Because we don't live in a world where I can stop working when my brain isn't. I can't stop just because I feel like I'm dying. I have to keep going.

So I do. We all do. You might not know it, but we do.

––––––

An earlier version of this chapter first appeared as a column in *Chronicle Vitae* on Nov. 20, 2015.

1. Honor Whiteman, "Depression affects memory by 'impairing ability to differentiate similarities,'" *Medical News Today*, Oct. 5, 2013. Retrieved from: http://www.medicalnewstoday.com/articles/267039.php.

ROUGH ACCOMMODATIONS

I taught at the university level for twelve years without ever considering seeking disability accommodations. (My disability is invisible, by the way—to those I've not disclosed to, my disability is imperceptible *as a disability*. People often think I'm weird, but they don't *necessarily* think I'm disabled.)

Even though I have a disability that would be legally recognized, even though I have a disability that costs me a great sum of money to treat each year, one that takes a great deal of effort to manage, I never considered reaching out to my institution's human resources department for accommodations.

Colleges and universities seem far more inclined to serve students with disabilities than faculty and staff with disabilities. Part of the reason why stems from the legal forces at play. Students and faculty are protected by different laws, which means that schools must comply with different legal pressures. Students are protected by a whole host of laws designed just for them. Faculty, on the other hand, are protected by different laws

—the same laws that protect any other employee in any other job.

It's fine, of course, that the legal protections for disabled faculty and staff are the same as for any other disabled employee at any other job, except that—everywhere—these legal protections are generally poorly enforced and difficult to access.

Moreover, disabled people in academia (like disabled people in any profession) face profession-specific challenges. Our colleagues struggle to avoid ableism. Attending academic conferences is almost always a challenge. The particulars of the academic job market—the conferences, the campus interviews—are challenging for disabled faculty. Furthermore, an institution's compliance with disability employment law rarely ensures the eradication of these profession-specific challenges.

What does it mean when an institution states that they will "comply" with disability law? Think about what the word "comply" means. It means that they will do only what they must, and only because they are forced to. Compliance means that, actually, they wish you wouldn't come to them and ask them to accommodate your needs as a person with a disability. It means that the onus is on you, the disabled person, to force an institution to comply at all.

Despite these challenges, filing for faculty and staff accommodations isn't a choice for many disabled workers in higher education, whether they have physical or psychiatric disabilities. Some disabled people choose to file for accommodations; but some disabled people *must*.

———

FILING for psychiatric disability accommodations as a college faculty or staff member is fraught for many reasons.

First, you are, even if just a little bit, exposing yourself as disabled, something that many faculty and staff do not want to do for fear of stigma—especially the particular stigma that members of the academy experience. Second, faculty and staff members are often discouraged (either latently or patently) from filing for accommodations for psychiatric disabilities. In Chapter 2, for example, I discuss how some of this latent hostility in the academy circulates. And third, campus disability offices are often—usually—designed with students in mind, not faculty.

(Before we go any further, I want to enter very big caveat: I know people who work in student disability support services all over this country. Many are doing amazing, I would go so far to say saintly, work.)

Here's what happened, for example, when I tried to figure out how to file for disability support at my own former institution, the University of North Carolina at Chapel Hill.

One morning, I typed these words into a search engine: "UNC Disability Accommodations." The very first webpage I saw seemed promising: "Accessibility Resources & Service," with an easy-to-remember URL (accessibility.unc.edu). I clicked the link, but when I arrived at the pretty website, my heart sank. It was for an office of the university's student-affairs division. "Fostering Student Learning and Success," the tagline read, right across the top banner.

I was not a student. I was a professor.

The first sentence of the site's Welcome page read,

"Accessibility Resources & Service, an office within The Division of Student Affairs, works with colleagues throughout the University to ensure that the programs and facilities of the University are accessible to all students." As a faculty member looking to file for disability accommodations, that website did not seem to be the right place for me. But then I saw a link on the main menu titled "For Faculty." Eager, I clicked it.

Disappointment again. The information on that particular page was about how faculty should interact with students with disabilities. Helpful in other circumstances, but not these.

Next, I tried the search bar at the top of the "Accessibility Resources & Service" page. I typed these words: "Faculty with Disabilities." No results.

I left the website and went back to the search engine. I typed a search with limiters: "UNC 'faculty with disabilities.'" No hits. Not a single one.

I'm not a total newbie to academic employment. I figured my next step would be to call human resources on the phone and explain to the total stranger who answered that I wished to file for disability accommodations. There would most likely have been uncomfortable questions, such as, "What kind of disability? What kind of accommodations?"

Those are questions that even I was not willing to discuss with a total stranger in HR right then.

There is a way to find an answer to my question: How do faculty and staff at my institution—or any institution—file for disability accommodations? The problem is that it is just much harder than it should be to find that answer.

While assistance to students with disabilities is front-and-center in university media—the glossy website, the search engine optimization—assistance to faculty with disabilities is comparatively invisible. At least at my top-tier research university.

Of course, I'm a lawyer and journalist who covers higher ed, so I know that the Equal Opportunity office handles accommodations (eoc.unc.edu). I navigated straight there, and sure enough, they have a tab for "accommodations." What followed after I clicked the tab was a list of steps so burdensome that anyone who has any choice would opt not to file. The language was rife with mistrust—"Eligibility is based on documented clinical data, not just self report or evidence of diagnosis." Disabled employees must sign a medical release so that the HR investigator has access to all of her medical records. And more.

This pattern of mistrusting disabled people is at the root of my rejection of the accommodations services I encounter. I just don't want to deal with suspicious people who have power over my livelihood. And since I have always had a choice—a privilege of many of us who are invisibly disabled—I have, thus far, avoided those suspicious people.

But let's not rely on my sample of 1. Let's see how other faculty feel about filing for accommodations for their psychiatric disabilities at their institutions.

———

JOAN: SOON TO BE ON THE JOB MARKET

Joan (a pseudonym) is a Ph.D. candidate in mathematics just entering the job market. She also has multiple psychiatric disabilities. One in particular affects her sleep, making it difficult for her to teach early morning classes. She's far less worried about finding a job—even in this market—than she is about finding a job that won't make her sick.

For example, she told me, "I need to know that I can have a reasonable schedule before I take a job, because the cost (to my health) of a bad schedule is high." But how can she possibly ask about class scheduling in an interview without bringing up her disability?

I got to know Joan because she emailed me out of the blue after reading a column I wrote for *Chronicle Vitae* on mental health and higher ed. She asked me this very question. She had no one else to turn to for advice, so she sought out mine.

She described how her field is particularly disabling: "Mathematics people are especially prone to an attitude that is fairly common in academia: that anyone who isn't a 'morning person' is lazy and can't possibly be good at his/her job." This attitude arises in particular around course scheduling. In her field, she said, requests "to avoid early morning classes often trigger disapproval from people with this attitude."

As a result of such negative reactions, she said: "Before my diagnosis, I spent several years feeling like a horrible, worthless person. ... And I am still afraid of encountering [this attitude] and being thought of as 'less,' simply because I don't bounce out of bed at 5 a.m., cheerful and ready to go."

I'm not sure on what planet sleeping past 5 a.m. is considered lazy, but Joan is making a serious point here. The hostile judgment of her peers and superiors in the past has made her afraid to disclose her disability on the job market now, or to even ask questions of potential employers to see if jobs would be a good fit for her, given her disabilities.

So what is Joan supposed to do? "I don't want to take a job offer without asking enough questions about accommodations and then be miserable (or worse) because they can't give me what I need with respect to scheduling and facilities." She added: "How do I make sure that a place I like can take care of me, without scaring them off with strange questions [before accepting an offer]?"

It is rare that there are safe structures in place to help a person like Joan navigate her department, the job market, or her new institution as a new faculty member. This lack of safe structures is a serious problem.

———

SHERRY: TENURED AND IN A TOP ADMINISTRATIVE POSITION

Sherry (a pseudonym) is in a very different position than Joan, yet faces remarkably similar challenges when it comes to finding structural help with her psychiatric disability. She is an associate professor at a university, a university with multiple divisions. Recently, she took a 12-month, administrative post to lend more stability to her life. This post makes her visible across all divisions on campus.

About 15 years ago, Sherry was diagnosed with bipolar disorder and treatment worked well, for the most part. Indeed, she told no one about her diagnosis, she said, "until after getting tenure, since the process of tenure landed me in the hospital and I had to tell my chair because it was in the middle of the semester." More recently, she had a reaction to her medication and had to be hospitalized again. But despite these two manifestations of her disability, she lives what one might consider a normal life.

A couple of people in her department know about her disability, but because it can be kept invisible and is highly stigmatized in society, Sherry keeps it private. Her institution considers bipolar disorder a "protected condition," but Sherry said she would never consider filing for disability accommodations even though filing could be a great benefit for her. "For example, if I had to be hospitalized for an extended period," she said, "I could claim bipolar as a disability and get disability leave." She believes the risks of seeking accommodations outweigh the benefits. Due to her administrative position, she's "now more visible, and that visibility comes with a need to protect myself."

After all, she tells me, "Who wants to publicly identify as [bipolar], especially in a high profile position? Not me."

I can identify with Sherry. Instead of requesting accommodations for bipolar disorder, I've spent my entire career forcing myself to do the accommodating, to fit myself around the parameters of my working conditions.

But Sherry and I, and others like us, are hardly the only ones. In a recent issue of *Profession*, the Modern Language Association's professional magazine, a group of disabled scholars reacted to the 2012 American Association of University Professors (AAUP) report on disability, "Accommodating Faculty Members Who Have Disabilities."[1] For those interested in ways forward for faculty and staff on university campuses, the MLA essays, titled "Faculty Members, Accommodation, and Access in Higher Education," are a great place to start.

PRIVACY INVADED

Susan Ghiaciuc, a professor at James Madison University and contributor to the MLA essay collection, described officially disclosing her multiple sclerosis to her employer. She writes that she "felt like an amateur actuary preparing a predictive model of my life to protect my employer against future loss." She had to provide lots of private information, including doctors' letters and more. "That this thorough burden of proof seemed legitimate didn't make it feel any less stressful or intrusive." Indeed, she writes that "the documentation I was required to provide once I disclosed my disability made me feel that I was being forced to put my various symptoms on display for public examination." Ghiaciuc argues that this hurdle will surely cause other academics to avoid disclosure.

The invasion of privacy Ghiaciuc describes is precisely why I never sought accommodations. I did not want my medical records in the hands of a revolving door of strangers in human resources. I did not want my diagnosis, my symptoms, my history, to become the property of my employer—especially when I was fairly certain, as both a lawyer and a veteran of academia, that no effective changes would be made. When weighing the costs against the benefits, the costs were just too high.

————

BURDEN MISPLACED

Brenda Jo Brueggemann, a professor at the University of Connecticut and another contributor to the MLA essay collection, puts her finger on the problem: "[The AAUP report] overindividualizes (yet again) the person with a disability as the problem, the burden, the issue. Stigma, disclosure, risk, the academic environment—all these are missing from the document." When the onus of righting disability wrongs in the workplace is on the disabled person, you have a problem.

This onus includes, for example, having to reveal highly personal medical information, as Ghiaciuc described—a process that everyone takes for granted as "just the way it is," legally, and as a way to avoid fraud. This fear of fraud reveals a presumption about disabled people, including disabled students, that all ableds must confront: that disabled people are fakers and malingerers, or milking the system for handouts. And this fear of fraud has a terrible side-effect: rather than screening out fakers, it keeps out disabled people who are afraid to submit themselves to inquisitions.

When Brueggemann mentions "stigma," "disclosure," and "risk," she takes on issues that attach to asking for disability accommodations, and how seeking accommodations, for some of us, seems like a really bad trade. In the context of higher education, giving up our privacy just might not be worth it. (Again, I'm writing from the privileged position of a person whose disability is invisible. Not all disabled people have the choice I had to not disclose.)

When Brueggemann talks about stigma, disclosure, and risk, she's talking about risking stigma by putting your disability at the center of your identity. You risk becoming no longer you in the eyes of others, but rather disabled-you. And for many in higher education, that risk is just too high.

―――――

WHERE DO WE GO FROM HERE?

Now, after leaving academia, I am mostly public with my otherwise invisible disability. But back when I worked for a university, I would never have considered filing for accommodations. As Ghiaciuc and Brueggemann describe, the process is too invasive and humiliating, and the rewards too paltry.

That is a structural problem that needs fixing. Here are some ideas for what to do about it.

First, since we're trained researchers, and this is what we're really good at, we're going to study the problem. In 2013-14, a team of disability-studies researchers led by Stephanie Kerschbaum and Margaret Price conducted an anonymous survey of faculty members with psychiatric disabilities. Over 400 academics in a variety of positions and from a variety of institutions took the survey. The team analyzed the results, focusing especially on faculty members' experiences disclosing their disabilities, and what barriers and supports existed for them if they sought accommodations. The team published their findings in 2017 in *Promoting Supportive Academic Environments for Faculty with Mental Illnesses: Resource Guide and Suggestions for Practice.*[2] We need more research, sure, but this document is a great start. Everyone should read it, and implement its suggestions. What an incredible change that would be.

Second, we're going to talk about the problem. People like Joan, the Ph.D. candidate in mathematics who was about to enter the job market, are out there, right now, in your departments. They are your graduate students and untenured colleagues. They don't know what to do. They're emailing complete strangers (i.e., me) who write things on the Internet to ask me for advice because they think they have no one else to turn to. That's not a good system. We need better support and mentoring in academia to prevent academics with disabilities from dropping out altogether or from getting sick or even dying.

Which leads me to point three. This is on all of us: We're going to actively make academia a safer, more welcoming place to be a faculty member with disabilities, including psychiatric disabilities. We'll stop making ableist insults, for example. (I talk about ableist insults in Chapter 2.) We'll learn why we have little to fear from our friends with bipolar disorder and schizophrenia—despite what the National Rifle Association wants us to think.

That's the only way to stop the fear and the self-doubt that transforms merely having a psychiatric disability into an epic sense of isolation.

———

An earlier version of this chapter first appeared as columns in *Chronicle Vitae* on Nov. 20, 2014, and in *Women in Higher Education* on Mar. 29, 2017.

1. Stephanie L. Kerschbaum et al., "Faculty Members, Accommodation, and Access in Higher Education," *Profession*, Dec. 9, 2013.
2. Margaret Price and Stephanie L. Kerschbaum, *Promoting Supportive Academic Environments for Faculty with Mental Illnesses: Resource Guide and Suggestions for Practice*, Jan. 2017. Retrieved from http://tucollaborative.org/sdm_downloads/promoting-supportive-academic-environments-for-faculty-with-mental-illnesses-resource-guide-and-suggestions-for-practice/.

REVISITING DISCLOSURE

I opened this book with a chapter called "Disclosure Blues," in which I concluded that it would be "hard for me to suggest that graduate students, contingent faculty, or pre-tenure faculty disclose their mental illnesses to their academic colleagues." The risks of such disclosure were just too great. In its original life, that chapter was the first column I'd ever written on mental health in academia.

In the years since I wrote that piece, much has changed in my life. I've left academia. I've also taken more steps to publicly disclose my own psychiatric disability, mostly in online essays, and now, in this book. In the wake of those disclosures, I've experienced some online trolling and other abuse, but not that much. I've done things to protect myself—for example, I liberally use the "block" function on Twitter, and I've left all comments on my blog disabled.

But now more than ever, higher ed workers—especially contingent instructors, alternative academic employees, early career faculty, or graduate students—come to me for advice about managing the effects of their own psychiatric disabilities on their careers. The more open I've become about my condition, the more others have sought me out as a resource. For that reason alone, disclosure has been a valuable choice for me.

After all, if I can serve as a positive model in which one's mental health (a) isn't a source of shame or (b) isn't shoved aside, but rather is a central part of one's health and well being, then I'm glad to take a little flack from ignorant trolls who are really just afraid of people with psychiatric disabilities and choose to express that fear with anger.

FINALLY FREE TO WRITE

Now that I've left the academy, one of the most amazing things about disclosing my mental illness—I have bipolar disorder—is that I have the opportunity to research and write about my expertise in disability studies. Academia never offered me any financial or professional support to do so during my time as a contingent faculty member. When I published articles and presented at conferences on disability studies, I did so, for the most part, on my own time and dime.

I worked for seven years as a writing instructor at an institution that contractually stated it would never hire me onto the tenure track. During that time, I was expected to teach my writing courses, grade stacks of papers, and conference with students multiple times each semester—all things that writing instructors know we must do to just keep up with the workload. (Prior to that, I worked for four years as a doctoral student doing pretty much the same thing.) But just because my institution crammed my time full of writing courses (and I added extra ones on other campuses to make ends meet) doesn't mean my research agenda up and died. I made time to research and write about psychiatric disability. Even after I left, I had two, maybe three, more articles coming out that final year—pieces I wrote and submitted on the academic publishing timeline when I was still teaching. (That timeline is, as you know, really, really slow.) But no institution I ever worked at supported my research in any way with time or money.

Although I miss the classroom, I don't miss being expected to robotically fulfill teaching requirements that my institution seemed to think could be met by whichever warm body walked through the door. I don't miss the way it treated my research as a "distraction." That life was the opposite of the life of the mind.

The irony is, back when I was teaching, I was terrified to disclose my psychiatric disability to anyone on the campus. My fears were many. There was, of course, the general expectation of mental perfection that all academics face, and the attendant desire of those of us with mental-health issues to hide our "broken brains." But I also struggled with a fear particular to contingent faculty—namely that, as I wrote in my first column, "everyone at work would learn about my secret disability, and that I would get fired because of it." I was also afraid of causing trouble as a person with a disability, in particular as a person with a stigmatized psychiatric condition. As I discussed in

Chapter 6, because of the stigma attached to my disability, I would never have asked for accommodations.

Given that new research shows that precarious academic employment itself is a risk factor for mental illness,[1] it seems like a terrible idea for someone with a psychiatric disability to take a contingent teaching job. It was just too bad that for seven years I never felt like I had a choice.

Now that I've left academia behind, not only have those fears fallen away (well, for the most part), but I now can devote myself to writing about disability studies, my area of specialty that I rarely had time for before.

PUTTING DISCLOSURE TO WORK

Disability studies is a youngish field that constantly examines the issue of disclosure.

Stephanie L. Kerschbaum, a rhetoric and disability studies scholar, in her work on "disclosing disability in academic writing," suggested that my disability cat was probably out of the bag anyway.[2] Kerschbaum writes that when "you do disability studies work, people assume that you either have a disability or that you are related to someone with a disability." She's not wrong. When I present on disability studies at conferences, I am often asked about my own relationship with disability. Sometimes, audience members ask me directly, "Are you disabled?"

When scholars in the field face personal questions about

their own disability status, Kerschbaum wonders, do those questions "reflect a kind of invasive curiosity about disability?"

Some queries do come from vulture-like questioners wanting to dig into your disabled body, she writes. But she also points out positive reasons to disclose disability—even in the context of academic writing (let alone in less-formal writing such as opinion-based journalism or personal essays)—that would give the writer more agency rather than less.

One reason she offered caught my eye in particular. Disclosure, she wrote, can provide "counternarratives that contest, resist, or challenge prevailing cultural assumptions about disability." In other words—as critical race theory, critical race feminism, and feminism have been observing for decades— telling your story in your own words is a great way to rebut someone else telling your story for you, and telling it wrongly.

———

REVISITING DISCLOSURE: WHOSE BURDEN?

But when telling your story includes discussing a highly stigmatized mental illness that would cause a majority of people to eye you with fear, what then? Do you disclose and allow your narrative to prove that you are not what the stigmatized stereotype says that you are? Do you let your testimony prove to the world that you are fully human and deserve to be treated humanely?

I don't know if disclosure can do all of this rhetorical work.

Sometimes that seems like too great of a burden for one's words to bear.

Perhaps the burden shouldn't be on people with mental-health issues to tell our stories for others to examine. Instead, perhaps we should all be asking ourselves some questions, like: When students or colleagues disclose that they have a psychiatric disability and need accommodations, what is our gut-level reaction? Is it one of sympathy? Or do we feel resentment that this person gets special treatment? Are we afraid of, or annoyed by, their quirks—that is, by the manifestations (if any) of their disabilities?

Or do we embrace the difference they bring to our departments and classrooms?

I'm willing to bet that "embracing difference" is not the common response. I'm willing to make that bet because of my own experiences, because of the reactions I get from my writing, and because of how colleagues (well, former colleagues) talk about mental illness when they don't know who is paying attention.

So to my non-tenure-track colleagues with psychiatric disabilities: Don't disclose, not yet. Let your counterparts with tenure handle this campaign for a while. Or leave it to people like me who are beyond the academic chopping block.

An earlier version of this chapter first appeared as a column in *Chronicle Vitae* on June 26, 2015.

1. Gretchen M. Reevy and Grace Deason, "Predictors of Depression, Stress, and Anxiety Among Non-Tenure Track Faculty," *Frontiers in Psychology*, July 7, 2014, doi: 10.3389/fpsyg.2014.00701.

2. Stephanie L. Kerschbaum, "On Rhetorical Agency and Disclosing Disability in Academic Writing," *Rhetoric Review*, 2014, Vol. 33, Issue 1, pages 55-71, DOI: 10.1080/07350198.2014.856730.

PART II
COLLEGIALITY

COLLEGIALITY AND DISABILITY

W ords matter. In higher education, by tradition, workers tend to refer to each other as "colleagues." In using that word, we signal that we value a collegial environment in which we share responsibility for a common mission. I would argue that a collegial environment is also one where colleagues share responsibility for one another.

But these days, it seems, the solitary, competitive, and even cutthroat nature of academic culture makes it unusually hard for collegiality to manifest. Academia has become a zero-sum game—which makes it more likely that faculty and staff will feel slighted, even cheated, when they believe someone else is getting something extra without merit. And who can blame them? The structure of higher education today makes everyone feel cheated. Sometimes that ire is turned on academics with disabilities who request accommodations. Rather than sharing responsibility for one another, some abled academics gossip and feel resentful toward their disabled colleagues. After all, if someone else is getting "more," then that means we must be getting "less," right?

Such resentment reveals itself outside the academy as well, of course. Anderson Cooper, of all people, reported a segment for 60 *Minutes* about how wasteful accommodations can be for businesses.[1] A business owner, however, does not profess to be the colleague of a person who wishes to purchase a widget.

But that's not how disability accommodations work. Accommodations are not a zero-sum game. Accessibility—the word I prefer to use in the place of "accommodations" when discussing creating an environment in which all people can thrive, normate and disabled alike—doesn't mean a disabled person is getting more. Accessibility means that our shared environment has become welcoming to all people, regardless of their ability.

Bad culture starts with training. Why do some academics resent colleagues with disabilities who seek accommodations? Some of that resentment can be attributed to the fact that we live in an ableist society. Some, however, can be attributed to the nature of doctoral training: We teach graduate students to suck it up and get by with less—and that those who can't suck it up aren't good enough to work in the academy. Later, when graduate students enter the academy as full-time workers, they carry those lessons with them.

I interviewed Jeri (a pseudonym), a doctoral student in the social sciences, who shared stories of how poorly she was treated as a disabled graduate student by faculty in her department. I've interviewed many other graduate students and former graduate students over the years, and their stories have much in common with Jeri's. In other words, she is not an outlier. Some of the ableism Jeri encountered was passive. For example, after a campus event, students and faculty would gather in a local bar or restaurant to talk, but those "drinking events" were not accessible or planned well. There was "no way to travel to get there," Jeri told me, and they were located off campus, making it hard for her to attend. It is difficult to form strong relationships with your colleagues when you are passively excluded from get-togethers and other professional events.

Some ableism Jeri encountered from faculty was more direct and insidious. For example, when working as a teaching assistant, she requested a chair in the classroom for her to sit in. That request "was seen as an insurmountable obstacle at first. Where would it come from? Who would pay?" We're talking about a chair, here. A chair shouldn't be a big deal. When departments make things like chairs a big deal, we make our disabled graduate students feel distinctly unwelcome.

Jeri was made to feel even more unwelcome by another faculty member who—despite the fact that Jeri already had experience as a teaching assistant—presumed that she "would be unable to TA because of her disability." Her negative experiences were not limited to run-ins with faculty. In one instance, she tried to explain to her fellow students why a software platform they were thinking about using for a project was not accessible. They had trouble believing her, despite her explanations, presuming that she was just uninformed because the platform "was certified by some association for the blind."

These interactions repeatedly sent the same message to Jeri:

She was a burden. "When I needed to ask for something new —
i.e., a chair — the response ... was, well, we've already done so
much for you, above and beyond what we do for the other
students." And that's the key here. She was made to feel that she
got more than she deserved. She was getting "above and
beyond" what other students got. She was getting unmerited
"special treatment." But those words reveal the problem with
how academic culture approaches accessibility. Accommodating
disabilities is not "special treatment." Making sure that a
classroom, a platform, or a department function is accessible to
all is not special treatment. And yet Jeri's faculty mentors and
student colleagues either passively or actively made her feel like
she didn't deserve any of the accommodations she needed to
simply be on an equal footing with her fellow students.

That kind of treatment alienates students with disabilities.
It also makes students who might need extra help—those who
are facing crises, even—keep those challenges to themselves. As
I explain later in this book, in Chapter 21, that's a risk we do not
want to take. Those of us with disabilities aren't asking for more
than we deserve; we are simply asking for what we need. As
colleagues, we should want to take responsibility for one
another. Doing so would make our departments healthier,
happier places to work. I know I sound Pollyannaish, but I'm
also right.

———

An earlier version of this chapter first appeared as a column in
Chronicle Vitae on February 7, 2017.

1. "Action Alert: Anderson Cooper's ADA Attack on 60 Minutes," *The Advocacy Monitor*, Dec. 7, 2016.

HELP! MY BEST FRIEND IS BIPOLAR

In this series on the academy and psychiatric disability, I wrote several columns that took on the issue of ableism and insensitivity in normates, i.e, nondisabled people. And, oh-so-predictably, in the posted comments to the columns and in responses on Twitter, certain readers have taken these essays to mean that I'm either: (1) enforcing political correctness (rather than humaneness toward others), (2) infringing on their right to free speech (because apparently I'm the State and have the power to enforce speech laws), or (3) making a mountain out of a molehill because why would anyone get offended by being called "totally bipolar" or "schizo"? (See Chapter 2, "She's So Schizophrenic!")

OK. If any of those characterize your view, you can just stop reading now. You are not my audience here. This particular chapter—indeed, this entire book—is for readers who want to be friends with people with psychiatric disabilities, with all disabled people. It's for people who want to be kind, thoughtful, and nice to disabled people. Who don't want to be jerks. Therefore, if being kind to disabled people does not sound like something that you want to be, just go away. I'm sure there's a 4chan someplace for people who agree with you.

Without further disclaimers, then, here's how to be an ally to your disabled friends, in particular your friends who have psychiatric disabilities.

Here's the scene. Your friend has recently disclosed to you in a private fashion that she has a mental illness, one that is permanent, with a lot of stigma attached to it. Let's say she has bipolar disorder. She discloses her disability to you because she is your friend and wants to be honest and open about who she is. What do you do?

———

KEEP HER SECRET.

This advice should be obvious, but I have to say it anyway. Scientific research has shown that most Americans believe, without evidence, that people with major mental illnesses pose significant threats of violence. This irrational fear is one of the many reasons why people with psychiatric disabilities face stigma when they disclose their disabilities.

Your friend has trusted you with a secret that could hurt her career, her friendships, and more—in ways that you can't imagine. Keep her secret safe.

———

DON'T STUDY HER FOR SYMPTOMS.

Now that you know that your friend has bipolar disorder, you might want to do research. So get on PubMed and do some reading. Search other journals for articles by disability studies scholars to educate yourself about ableism and people with psychiatric disabilities. That's all really great.

But you can't turn your keen researcher's eye upon your friend's body, voice, and face and study her. She is not an object for you to learn from. Don't examine her symptoms, waiting for her to do something "bipolar." You would be objectifying her, which is weird and demeaning.

Plus, I can promise you, she'll be able to feel your eyes studying her. She'll be able to tell. And she'll hate you for it.

DON'T ASK HER IF SHE'S "TAKEN HER MEDS."

A former friend asked me this question one time. It happened shortly after I was diagnosed with my disability. I shared my secret with my best friend in the world, who was also my first roommate after college.

Shortly after I shared my secret with her, we had a disagreement about something I can't even remember now. She asked, in the heat of the disagreement, "Do you need to take your medicine?" She spoke as though the only reason I could possibly be disagreeing with her was because I was unmedicated, as though I was acting erratic or unstable.

I could have wept at the betrayal.

We'd been friends for many years at that point, but that was the first time I'd felt betrayed by her. How could I ever again trust someone who had attributed my thoughts, my very observations about the world—especially the ones that disagreed with hers—to a broken brain?

Now, twenty years later, the one thing I remember about her is that one moment—the moment she made me feel like a freak for being different.

Don't do that.

———

DO REMIND YOUR FRIEND TO TAKE HER MEDICINE, IF SHE ASKS YOU TO.

Wait, you're thinking. Isn't this advice the opposite of what you just said? No. The point is, your friend with bipolar disorder gets to decide—not you—whom she talks with about her medicine. If she lets you into that circle of people, count yourself lucky. It's a tiny group.

I was at an academic conference recently. Before I left, my husband hurt his hand badly. I was worried about leaving him at that point but, at his urging, ultimately decided to attend the meeting. Then, once my colleague, Ariane (a pseudonym), and I arrived at the conference hotel, I got a call from my husband. His hand was worse, and he was headed to an emergency doctor. Being me, and knowing what I knew about his injury, I was thinking of compartment syndrome, of amputation. And pretty soon I wasn't thinking at all.

If I'd been at home, I would have been advocating for my husband, ensuring he got the best medical care. But there I was, out of state at a stupid academic conference and completely unable to help. Paralyzed. Panicked. Tortured. Frozen.

Ariane is someone I trust. She knows me, and she knows about my disability. She has my permission to help care for me, even when that care includes talking about my medication. She said to me, "You need to take [insert specific drug name here], and you need to eat. Let's make that happen." So we did.

I calmed down, my body relaxed—after receiving its first real meal of the day—and a couple of hours later my husband called to tell me that the treatment he received worked. Everything would be OK with his hand.

If you are lucky enough to be given the level of trust by your own friend that I give to Ariane, you are lucky indeed.

I count myself lucky, too. Ariane might very well save my life some day.

————

DO ASK IF THERE ARE SITUATIONS THAT ARE HARD FOR YOUR FRIEND BECAUSE OF HER DISABILITY, AND THEN BE SENSITIVE TO THOSE SITUATIONS.

This rule calls upon all of your empathetic reserves. Be warned: It's going to be hard sometimes. Your friend may need your help at unpredictable moments and in unpredictable ways. Part of having a psychiatric disability means that sometimes a person's brain can react in unexpected ways to stimuli—unexpected even to the person with the disability. Here's an example.

Recently, I had to host and give a talk at a conference. Like most of you, I've given dozens of talks. This day shouldn't have been a big deal. Indeed, that very morning, I ran into a former student of mine, and she asked me if I was nervous about my talk. I actually told her, "I don't get nervous." But a confluence of circumstances caused me to eat those words. I didn't get nervous in the way that most people would recognize—no sweaty palms or shyness. Instead, I felt panicked, as though there were an assassin in the building trying to kill me, but I didn't know who it was. Being there became physically painful.

Now, I did my level best to make sure that no one knew that I felt that way. And I'm sure that anyone who was there and is reading this now would think that this sort of reaction—the pain of panic—at my own conference is a little nuts.

Guess what. "Nuts" is correct, if a little colloquial. Even I couldn't have predicted that I'd have this reaction. But I had it nonetheless: hands shaking, blurting out inappropriate words now and then (fortunately not into the microphone), forgetting guests' names, and generally losing my cool in unexpected ways. I warned the two people who knew anything about my disability that I was feeling this way. They covered for me as best they could. Sat next to me at the dinner. Gave the opening and closing remarks solo while I stood silent, pretending that this was the plan all along.

Believe me—if I weren't the host—heck, if my talk weren't the second-to-last one of the entire day—I would have claimed a stomach virus and left early. Instead, I was trapped in a room where I felt as though my skin were being pulled off in strips, and slowly.

I hosted the conference. I gave my talk. It was torture, but I did my job.

The only thing—the only thing—that could possibly help me through something like that is a friend by my side, whispering in my ear, You will be OK. You will be OK.

You have a chance to be that friend.

———

An earlier version of this chapter first appeared as a column in *Chronicle Vitae* on Jan. 2, 2015.

HANDLING PERSONAL TRAGEDIES AROUND YOU

In academia, as in any workplace, you encounter the personal tragedies of the people around you. Colleagues experience illness, divorce, death, and more. As much as anything I've written about in this series, those traumatic events interrupt the life of the mind.

Academics lead uniquely solitary work lives. Yet at the same time, we are uniquely tied to our work—and therefore to our colleagues. For example, we form long-lasting relationships across time and space: We stay in touch with our advisers and fellow students long after leaving graduate school behind. Our fields tend to be closed universes in which relationships grow across institutions, states, and national borders.

All of which means that, in many ways, academia is like an extended family, not just a job. For the sake of our extended academic families, I decided to learn more about how to react better to personal tragedies in our midst. I reached out to two academic professionals who have experienced significant personal tragedies during their careers. What I learned from interviewing these two academic professionals is this: like most workplaces, higher education has a ways to go when it comes to figuring out how best to care for those who suffer tragedies within its esteemed walls.

It's normal to have trouble saying the right thing when someone near you is suffering. The academics I interviewed have not only shared their stories, but they also gave some simple guidelines to help make things easier for all of us when the time comes to support our own colleagues.

―――――

NO OSTRICHES—OR, DON'T FEAR PEOPLES' PAIN

The simplest way to explain the No Ostriches guideline is this: Don't be afraid to say words like "sick" or "died." Speak plainly to people who are suffering. Don't skate around their pain.

Speaking plainly about personal tragedies might take practice. It can be hard to say things like, "I'm so sorry to hear that your wife died." Those aren't words most people are accustomed to saying. Euphemisms might seem easier. But the person who is suffering isn't living a euphemism. You will probably need to practice the difficult words before you speak to a grieving spouse or parent, before you speak to the person diagnosed with cancer.

Soon after Adeline (a pseudonym) began her academic career, her son died unexpectedly. Before that heartbreaking tragedy, Adeline told me, she used to make the ostrich mistake just like everyone else: "I was completely afraid of mentioning the unmentionable as though me not mentioning it meant that it didn't exist."

After her son's death, she learned what a problem silence can be. Hiding from personal tragedies, she said, "creates a situation in which the person experiencing loss or suffering ceases to exist, because people stop talking to you, afraid of what they might say, fearing that it will upset you—as though you weren't already upset, or their ignoring your presence wasn't upsetting."

Many people didn't know what to say to Adeline about her son's death. So they said nothing at all. And by saying nothing to her, she felt like she completely disappeared when she needed others most.

Adeline did encounter "a rare handful of people who knew how to handle such tragedy." This small group had been taught by parents who had experienced death, for example, and knew how to face it head-on. "Most people are simply ill-equipped," she said, "a state that is culturally reinforced." From her own experience before her son's death, she knows that "we come by this awkwardness with death honestly. We are not taught well."

But there was another aspect of fear that Adeline encountered—fear of the tragedy itself. Adeline told me, "I felt like I was an object of pity (not that I could argue with this stance, since it was all indeed quite pitiful), but gazes were averted to avoid having to face one's worst fear, as though my person became the embodiment of those fears." I'm sure most parents reading this chapter would agree that having a child die is indeed their worst nightmare. But, as Adeline experienced, her colleagues and friends sought to escape their worst fear by escaping from her, with horrible consequences: "So to hide from me, in order to hide from yourself, means I become invisible and totally alone."

As you can see, at a time when Adeline most needed her colleagues' support, they were most unable to give it.

Rachel (a pseudonym) suffered a different sort of personal crisis. In graduate school, she spent nearly a month in the hospital after a neurological trauma. She received lots of visitors, which she thought "was great until I went back to work and realized just how many people had seen me disheveled and bra-less." Based on that experience, Rachel added a corollary to the No Ostriches rule: the No Vultures rule. It goes like this: Help protect anyone enmeshed in a tragedy from those who might just want to stare out of grim fascination—to pick over the bones, so to speak.

As a graduate teaching assistant at the time, Rachel was one of the lowest-ranking members of her department. Once she returned to work, she felt exposed by her hospital stay and illness. In retrospect, she thinks that "people in a position of authority should send flowers, or messages with others, and then stay away until they are invited in." Her boss, for example, could have waited until Rachel was clean, and up and about, before coming to visit.

Birds aside, Rachel emphasizes: "Don't be afraid to be human." One of the most prominent members of the faculty reached out to her shortly after her return to work. Rachel describes the moment with joy: "If this professor could not only come into TA offices (where professors rarely went), but also give me a hug, and tell me to call him at home anytime, then I am pretty sure anyone can."

———

DON'T MAKE PRESUMPTIONS—OR, ASK WHAT PEOPLE NEED

We often make presumptions about what someone in a personal crisis needs—and those presumptions are often incorrect. These presumptions may serve only to make us feel better, not the actual person suffering. We tell ourselves things like, "He needs to be alone right now, so I'll just stay away." We take control away from the person in need in order to comfort ourselves.

Adeline notes that, after her son's death, "I found myself wishing for a Victorian year of black dress, or a black armband to indicate to outsiders that I was in an abnormal state: Tread lightly." She thought that an external marker would help others treat her with more care while she was dealing with the loss of her child.

But Adeline discovered she was wrong. An external marker would likely have made no difference. She met for lunch with a friend who had survived breast cancer. "I'm embarrassed to admit," Adeline said, "I actually felt jealous that her pain and anguish were visible, marked on her body by hair loss and sickness." But then she had a surprise: "I asked her if these visible markers were helpful, and she said, No." Adeline had thought those markers would spur people to reach out to help, rather than turn away. But instead, Adeline's friend felt as alone with her cancer as Adeline did with her son's death. In fact, strangers—not friends—most often recognized the markers of cancer and offered comfort.

After her hospital stay, Rachel also had to deal with the incorrect presumptions of colleagues about what she needed. Her challenge came in the form of presumptions about what she was—and was not—able to do at work. Some hard-earned work responsibilities were taken away from her without her consent. Losing those responsibilities felt patronizing and even degrading, especially after she had worked so hard to regain her standing in the department. She felt particularly vulnerable that her injury was to her brain.

It seemed, she said, like everyone believed she needed to be coddled: "She needs to recover, so I am going to determine what she is and isn't capable of." In many ways, then, Rachel's problem was simply one of communication, and it would have been easily overcome had her colleagues simply asked her what she needed, instead of taking her decisions away from her.

GIVE COMFORT—NEVER DEMAND IT FOR YOURSELF

In "How Not To Say the Wrong Thing," Susan Silk and Barry Goldman propose the "Dump-Out" rule of comforting others.[1] This is the rule's basic premise: You cannot expect someone who is suffering to comfort you. Instead, you should comfort those who are closest to the trauma, and dump your own suffering on those who are farther away from it than you are.

Silk and Goldman even drew a nice illustration consisting of concentric rings to show how this "Kvetching Order" works. Comfort In. Dump Out.

When Adeline's son died, people "dumped in" on hurt. They turned to her for comfort for their own grief about his death, as though, absurdly, anyone's grief could trump a parent's. Adeline has a theory about why we tend to focus on ourselves when faced with someone else's pain: "The only socially viable avenue of discourse about death and loss takes the form of sharing one's own personal pain."

But today, years later, Adeline continues to find it necessary to take care of others around her when the subject of her son's death arises: "Even now, I work hard to help people avoid falling into my landmine of conversation. If I sense questions in the hall tending toward the subject of family, then I gently move the conversation back to the academic, fearing that I might have to explain: No, I don't have kids. I did. But not anymore." As her listeners figure out what she means, that she has a child who died, she tells me, "I cannot abide their pain as well as my own." And Adeline has learned that her listeners don't know how to avoid putting their pain onto her.

Rachel sums up her similar experience succinctly: "If you can't deal, don't visit." She lost a friendship because her friend couldn't cope with Rachel's illness. "I remember her palpable sense of discomfort, horror, loss, pity," she said. "I knew nothing would be the same. Even if I had a full recovery, she was never going to see me the same way." This was a colleague Rachel had trusted, a junior faculty member she looked up to as a mentor and spent time with as a friend. She can't remember the last time she and this former friend spoke—because Rachel's illness was too hard for her friend to deal with. That's a classic case of dumping in the wrong direction.

As Rachel's and Adeline's stories show, it's not that hard to comfort our friends and colleagues who suffer personal tragedies. We just need to learn what to do. Keeping these three basic guidelines in mind will go a long way toward making higher education a more humane place.

———

An earlier version of this chapter first appeared as a column in *Chronicle Vitae* on April 16, 2015.

1. Susan Silk and Barry Goldman, "How Not To Say the Wrong Thing," *Los Angeles Times*, April 7, 2013.

I'M NOT BRAVE

When I first started writing publicly about my psychiatric disability (i.e., mental illness), I received messages via Facebook, Twitter, and email from normates praising my "bravery." I was taken by surprise. They were calling me brave for disclosing something I've lived with every day for decades.

I think I was supposed to say "thank you." But I didn't feel thankful for those comments. I felt crabby, and then guilty for feeling crabby. So I did some research trying to figure out if I was alone in how I felt.

Apparently, calling a person with psychiatric disabilities "brave" is a pattern, a trend. Take a look at similar pieces by academics like Elyn Saks in *The Chronicle of Higher Education*,[1] Lisa McElroy in *Slate*,[2] Brian Clarke on the *Faculty Lounge Blog*,[3] and Jacqui Shine in *Chronicle Vitae*.[4] Scroll through the comments or do a keyword search for the word "brave" and you'll see that "You're so brave" is a common theme in responses to academics publicly discussing their psychiatric disabilities. So what's the problem with that?

To be clear: I'm not talking about the furtive emails I receive from other disabled people telling me about their own mental illnesses that they wish they could disclose, but, for whatever reason, cannot. Those precious little notes often come from a void of loneliness, shot straight from one soul to another.

No. I'm talking about comments from nondisabled people telling me how courageous and inspiring they think my words are.

Which leads me to the first problem with the "you're so brave" response.

———

PROBLEM NO. 1: IT SOUNDS A LOT LIKE "INSPIRATION PORN."

Normates who call you brave for disclosing a disability often feel "inspired" by you as well. Like this: "Your bravery in sharing your psychiatric disability with the world is so inspiring." (That's not an actual quotation from a message I received. Not, you know, *exactly*.) "Brave" plus "inspiration" when directed at a disabled person is a double-whammy of terrible. As the late, brilliant disability activist Stella Young so nicely put it, "We're not here for your inspiration."[5]

Young, who was a disability activist and all-around ass-kicker, launched a full-scale attack on "inspiration porn" via a TED Talk and more. According to Young, inspiration porn "is an image of a person with a disability, often a kid, doing something completely ordinary—like playing, talking, running, drawing a picture, or hitting a tennis ball—and carrying a caption like 'your excuse is invalid' or 'before you quit, try.'"

Why create inspiration porn? Young explains: "[I]t's there so that nondisabled people can put their worries into perspective. So they can go, 'Oh, well, if that kid who doesn't have any legs can smile ... I should never, ever feel bad about my life.'" Inspiration porn lets nondisabled people objectify people with disabilities, and through that objectification, feel better about themselves.

If a nondisabled person calls me brave, that person is invoking the inspiration narrative, implying that I've overcome a challenge (such as fear of the stigma against mental illness) in publicly disclosing my disability. But here's the thing: I'm a disability studies scholar, and a writer, and so writing about disability isn't that weird for me. There was no "overcoming" here. If my columns are meant to inspire anything, they're meant to inspire the nondisabled to stop treating the disabled so terribly.

But you know what? Even if it *were* brave of me to disclose my mental illness in a public venue, I'm not here for your inspiration. Please don't put that burden on me—some days I don't feel brave at all. Some days, just like everyone else, I don't want to get out of bed.

When you foist such expectations upon a writer just because he or she has a disability, you are imposing too much.

Indeed, that imposition itself is stigma. Which leads me to problem No. 2.

———

PROBLEM NO. 2: IT PILES ON—RATHER THAN FIGHTS—
STIGMA.

Quickly, answer me this: Why would a person be brave for
disclosing a psychiatric disability?

Your gut answer would probably be something like:
Psychiatric disability is stigmatized in our society. Publicly
revealing that you have one takes great courage because you are
likely bringing that stigma upon yourself.

Right?

When you call a person brave for disclosing a psychiatric
disability, your gut answer becomes truth.

When people called me brave after I disclosed my own
disability, they made big presumptions about me. They
presumed that publishing that piece caused me to feel the
effects of societal stigma. They presumed that I'd internalized
those negative perceptions in certain ways. But stigma is not
monolithic. We all experience it in different ways on different
days—and we react to it differently, too.

Stigma is not just about being afraid to be yourself, but
calling people with a mental illness "brave" implies that it is.

When I published my first column disclosing my
disability, I was not afraid of professional repercussions
(although I did, in the column, discuss an old fear that I used
to hold). But then I received literally dozens, perhaps
hundreds, of well-meaning messages calling me "brave" for
publishing it. And I thought, "Well, Katie, if all of these

people think you're so brave, *maybe you should be afraid of something.*"

Indeed, by insisting that it took "great courage" to talk about having a psychiatric disability, these message-writers inadvertently (well, let's hope so) imposed that fear upon me at a time when I might not have felt any at all. They were piling on more stigma and not giving me room to feel anger, frustration, annoyance, and all of the myriad emotional reactions to stigma that people with psychiatric disabilities may experience.

Which leads me to problem No. 3 about being called "brave."

————

PROBLEM NO. 3: IT STOPS, RATHER THAN STARTS, CONVERSATIONS.

You know what people with disabilities really don't like? Normates—especially those whose opinions we did not ask for—telling us what must be going on inside our brains. They probably meant well, but my brain is already kind of a sensitive subject (see, e.g., stigma), and now I'm getting emails from total strangers telling me how much they know about my feelings.

So instead of making assumptions—which can halt conversation—try asking questions. I do have reasons for talking about psychiatric disability, stigma, and yes, fear—even fear that I used to and still sometimes feel—but please don't assume that you know what I'm feeling when you couldn't possibly know unless you know me.

If you're reading this, you're likely an academic or former academic. Use your skills of inquiry and ask me: "How did you feel when you published this piece?" Or: "Did you feel afraid when you disclosed your disability?" And then I can explain.

Questions like these add to the discourse around a topic. They start conversations about psychiatric disability and the academy. And these conversations—how the academy does or does not deal with psychiatric disabilities—are important ones for all of us to have. Because whether we like it or not, psychiatric disability surrounds us in the academy every day.

———

An earlier version of this chapter first appeared as a column in *Chronicle Vitae* on Sept. 25, 2014.

1. Elyn R. Saks, "Mental Illness in Academe," *The Chronicle of Higher Education*, Nov. 25, 2009.
2. Lisa T. McElroy (now Tucker), "Worrying Enormously About Small Things," *Slate*, July 18, 2013.
3. Brian Clarke, "Law Professors, Law Students and Depression . . . A Story of Coming Out," *The Faculty Lounge*, March 31, 2014.
4. Jacqui Shine, "On Depression, and the Toll Academia Exacts," *Chronicle Vitae*, Dec. 18, 2013.
5. Stella Young, "We're Not Here for your Inspiration," July 2, 2012, ABC News (Australian Broadcasting Corporation).

NOT A COMPLIANT WOMAN COLLEAGUE

In July of 2016, Northwestern University banned from campus Professor Jacqueline Stevens, a female tenured professor of political science. The ban came after the dean of her college and the associate chair of her department suggested she was "erratic and uncivil" and was thus possibly a threat to campus safety.

Northwestern did not allow Professor Stevens to return to campus until she underwent a fitness-for-duty evaluation by a medical professional. The evaluation had to show that she was fit—mentally—to return to work. In September, Professor Stevens passed the evaluation and was reinstated.

Stevens published online the letter from her dean that banned her from campus. The adjectives used to describe her are interesting. Along with "erratic" and "uncivil," the dean also accuses her of being "threatening," "aggressive," "disruptive," "disrespectful," and—again—"uncivil."

By her own account and that of others, Professor Stevens

was an outspoken critic of her "institution and her colleagues." According to the *Chronicle of Higher Education*, she advised a student who sued the school and led a campaign to block a high-profile hire that she disagreed with.[1]

She was not—at all—a compliant woman colleague.

She most likely was aggressive, disruptive, disrespectful, and uncivil. To me, an outside reader of the various accounts of this conflict, the list of adjectives the dean used to describe her behavior—set alongside Professor Stevens's political disruptions on campus—seem to lead to a very disturbing conclusion.

The dean's letter reads like Professor Stevens was sent to the psychiatrist for being an angry woman.

———

LEST WE GLORIFY PROFESSOR STEVENS, she defended herself with incredibly ablest language in an interview with the *Chronicle of Higher Education*: "I have never been diagnosed with a mental illness, nor prescribed psychotropic medications, nor even had this suggested to me. ... It's not like I'm an unknown quantity and you can just run around and say that I'm a crazy person." She does, indeed, appear disrespectful.

What I want to ask here is this: Would a male professor who had been outspoken and critical of his campus and colleagues have been so easily branded as erratic and—let's be honest about the accusation—unstable?

I believe the answer is no. Men are permitted a much broader range of emotions—especially workplace emotions. Men are allowed to get angry at work, and women are not.

It all starts with the way men and women are expected to speak.

We saw it over and over again during the 2016 election season while Hillary Clinton ran on the Democratic Party ticket. In "Why Do So Many People Hate the Sound of Hillary Clinton's Voice?" Elspeth Reeve explains that women's voices get much harsher scrutiny than men's voices: "Men are supposed to be assertive, loud, and competitive. Women are supposed to be soft-spoken, cooperative, and helpful."[2]

Furthermore, Clinton's voice alienates people because it projects strength. A linguist explains (to Reeve): "There's nothing breathy about Hillary Clinton's voice. And if somebody doesn't want a woman to be powerful they're not going to like that voice."

A woman who speaks powerfully will be disliked simply for how she is speaking. A woman who is not soft-spoken or cooperative is breaking strongly coded gender rules. Whether she is running for president or arguing a point to her department chair, she has certain ways she is supposed to talk —culturally.

It is no wonder, then, that a colleague defending Professor Stevens's behavior in an interview with *The Chronicle of Higher Education*—a recent past president of Northwestern's Faculty Senate, a credible source—took pains to describe Professor Stevens as "not 'coarse or rude.'" Coarseness and rudeness are improper speech patterns for women. To be coarse or rude is enough, it seems, to get a woman branded as erratic and threatening.

A polite (read: sane) woman follows gender rules.

———

Women misbehaving and being branded as "crazy" for it is not a new thing. In an article in the journal *Victorian Studies*, "Victorian Women and Insanity," researcher Elaine Showalter pointed out these same connections in her now-famous study of Victorian asylums and gender disparities.[3]

For example, Showalter reports how female asylum inmates were often reported to be more vocal, rude, and disruptive than male inmates. However, "Such reports primarily reflect the expectations and wishes of male observers that women should be quiet, virtuous, and immobile."

In other words, it wasn't that the female asylum inmates were louder or crasser than the male inmates; it was that they broke the strict behavior rules for their gender.

Women in the workplace already have such a limited range of acceptable responses when they're angry or upset. Women are not supposed to show their anger, and when we do get angry —say, by raising our voices—our behavior can be perceived as so outside the norm that we are seen as out of control, as "erratic," as dangerous. (I described my own deep fear of that very word— erratic—in Chapter 1 of this book.)

However we feel about Professor Stevens's situation (I, for one, strongly dislike her ablest comments), we should be concerned about her treatment by her institution. We should be concerned that a university can so easily silence a female colleague by calling her crazy.

Such actions are both sexist (as I've discussed here) and harmful to those of us who have psychiatric disabilities.

———

An earlier version of this chapter first appeared as a column in *Women in Higher Education* on Nov. 1, 2016.

1. Robin Wilson, "Citing Safety Concerns, Northwestern U. Bans Tenured 'Gadfly' Professor From Campus," *The Chronicle of Higher Education*, Sept. 3, 2016.
2. Elspeth Reeve, "Why Do So Many People Hate the Sound of Hillary Clinton's Voice?" *The New Republic*, May 1, 2015.
3. Elaine Showalter, "Victorian Women and Insanity," *Victorian Studies*, Winter 1980, Vol. 23, No. 2, Pages 157-181.

CONFERENCE CHALLENGES FOR PEOPLE WITH PSYCHIATRIC DISABILITIES

For people with psychiatric disabilities, attending an academic conference can be hard in unexpected ways.

Usually, when we talk about helping people get what they need to make their way in the world—whatever their disability—the standard is "accommodation." That term connotes "doing something extra" to meet someone's needs. It should surprise no one that most disabled people, if they can find any sort of workaround, will avoid seeking official accommodations. We don't want to feel like our existence requires something extra—especially since getting that something extra requires interacting with gatekeepers, who often do not want to give us that extra thing. (For more about this kind suspicious of gatekeeping of disability accommodations, see Chapter 6, "Rough Accommodations," or Chapter 14, "Accessibility is for Everyone.")

That's the beauty of taking an "accessibility" approach to meeting people's needs. Accessibility is the idea that a space is always, one hundred percent of the time, welcoming to people with disabilities. With an accessibility approach, accommodations are integrated into a space—say, an annual conference—and not particularized to an individual. Most important, the burden shifts from the individual to society.

What does that mean for the particular challenges that people with psychiatric disabilities face in attending academic conferences?

People with psychiatric disabilities are not a monolithic group, because psychiatric disabilities manifest in a variety of ways. But I will give some examples to illustrate how certain changes in the physical and interpersonal qualities of academic conferences could—with little cost or effort—make those meetings more accessible for us.

My ideas on this front are aimed at making space for people who need space *away* from other people, even just for a moment. I'm talking about small changes that might be overlooked because they seem so inconsequential. But for someone like me—someone who wants to participate and who wants to be there, but can't be "on" for hours on end—these small things can make a big difference. And what you might find as you read these suggestions is that they apply to many people, even those who aren't disabled. That's the other great thing about the accessibility approach—it benefits everyone.

————

HALLWAY SEATING

The last conference I attended was a big one, with several thousand attendees, and it was held in a large conference center. There were four floors of conference space. The main lobby area had plenty of seating for its size, but the seating was almost always full. The second, third, and fourth floors were composed of wide hallways—like, really wide—and really long as well. Curiously, though, there was no seating in these really long, really wide hallways. If you needed to take a look at the program to find your next room, you simply had to stand. Imagine thousands of feet of hallway, and not a single place to sit.

The problem with that arrangement is this: Sitting connotes a private moment in a way that standing doesn't. While I've been standing, I've had total strangers approach me to strike up conversations. Yes, I'm at a convention, but sometimes I need a breather. I need to sit in semi-privacy, just for a moment, so that, after that break, I can keep going.

Conference organizers should make sure that plenty of chairs and benches are available outside of meeting rooms to provide a quiet place to sit and take a short break. The alternative was that we all had to stand there looking lost, fumbling with our things, and getting bumped into by crowds of people. We never had any breaks. And consequently, every day, I had to leave early, before the final sessions, because I was mentally exhausted.

———

SECRET STAIRCASES

Conference elevators are notoriously crowded. I have a friend who has severe claustrophobia. I have something similar. So I've become adept at discovering the secret staircases that lead from floor to floor. At the many hotels I've stayed in for meetings, I have never, ever seen another person in these staircases. It's weird. Most of the staircases exist as fire escapes—another reason I like to familiarize myself with them—but they're an excellent, private way to move around the conference space while taking small breaks at the same time.

The thing is, they're often not well marked. When I show the staircases to my fellow neurodivergents, they're amazed, relieved, and then annoyed. Why didn't they know about these staircases sooner? Why didn't they have access to this private, quiet way to get around that didn't require use of the horrid elevators? I don't have an answer. I just show them the doorways and where they lead.

Secret staircases are another way I balance my desire to participate in a crowded conference with a brain that overloads more easily than that of other people.

My suggestion for conference planners: It's as simple as hanging a sign. Like the Quiet Rooms that more and more conferences are finally figuring out are an important thing to have, signs could point the way to a "Quiet Staircase." Those few peaceful moments can make all the difference when you're neurodivergent at a massive conference.

———

NO MORE SHAMING FOR READING PAPERS ALOUD

This is a pet peeve of mine. Many speakers at conferences get slammed either in private (by gossips) or on social media (by what I would consider trolls) for reading their conference papers out loud on a panel.

Now, some presenters read their papers because they lack audience awareness. They read fast to cram in all of their oh-so-important ideas, or they read the paper because they just didn't prepare well. I'm not talking about these people right now.

I'm talking about another group of presenters—the ones who read their conference papers because they have to. Many of these people read their papers in a captivating manner. They have fabulous audience awareness. But they still read.

I am in this group of readers. We read because reading, itself, is an accessibility measure for us—for a whole host of reasons such as anxiety or disfluency. We read because doing so makes our participation at a conference possible. It's makes the conference accessible.

Don't shame presenters who read their papers. Don't tweet snarky comments with the conference hashtag, e.g., "Ugh stop reading papers already! #conference2016." First of all, we see those tweets. Second of all, you just might be attacking someone who reads because she doesn't have a choice.

———

An earlier version of this chapter first appeared as a column in *Chronicle Vitae* on April 28, 2016.

ACCESSIBILITY IS FOR EVERYONE

The law is quirky about language. When I was studying disability law in law school, I had to learn how to spell the term "accommodation" correctly—two Cs, two Ms. It is a long, arduous word, with lots of extra letters.

The word "judgment," alternatively, only contains one E when it is written by a lawyer. A sure way to tell whether a non-lawyer is doing the writing is by the insertion of an extra E after the G, like this: "judgement." A similar sign of a non-lawyer is an S in the abbreviation of "versus": lawyers write "v." whereas non-lawyers write "vs."

After I became a law professor, I gave my students this mnemonic:

Tyson vs. Holyfield—That's a boxing match.

Holyfield v. Tyson—That's an assault and battery claim arising from a particular injury to Holyfield's ear.

After a few years, of course, my students had no idea what

ear injury I was talking about. That particularly gory bout had slipped from the popular consciousness.

The point is, every term in law has its spelling, and with its spelling, its meaning, and with its meaning, its baggage.

Accommodation. A long, arduous word. And what does it mean? Meeting the needs of? Assisting? Making extra space for? That's it. It means extra. Doing something extra. Like its extra letters, the word itself implies extra work that most people do not want to be doing, but they do it because they have to.

———

AN ESSAY on Medium recently made the rounds, written by a disabled writer named Brittany Quinn.[1] In the essay, Quinn described a terrible experience at the Seattle Airport's TSA security checkpoint. Quinn has an invisible physical disability, and the TSA officers gave her some serious hassle about accommodating her. Among other things, she was met with suspicion and resistance to helping her: "The male [TSA] agent there was polite, but began explaining to me in a condescending fashion (with no prompting) that they would be happy to help me—IF I was telling them the truth about having a disability."

The problem, of course, was that we as a society approach disability as something to be accommodated. We create spaces that are inaccessible, and then we say, "Should someone with a disability need to enter here, we will make special accommodations so that they can." That's the deal with accommodations: they are always special, extra, more. A burden.

And when you are asking underpaid, overworked, annoyed (wouldn't you be?) federal employees to do something special, there is a high likelihood that they're not going to want to do something extra or take on more of a burden. Quinn, the author of the piece, joked about needing to wear her parking pass around her neck to prove she has a disability—to prove she deserves accommodation.

But what this incident proves is that our society's approach to disability is wrong from the get-go.

Accommodation is not accessibility.

If a space is accessible, that space is always, 100% of the time, welcoming to disabled people. Disabled people do not have to ask for anything. They do not have to prove they have disabilities. They do not have to interact with gatekeepers.

They can simply be.

———

IN SHORT, accommodation is not accessibility, and it is not nearly as good. Here's why.

"Accommodation" shifts the burden to the person with disabilities. Accommodation requires a person with a disability to interact with a gatekeeper, to ask for something extra, and to prove that she deserves accommodation in the first place—that she is "disabled enough."

Furthermore, many disabilities, physical, psychiatric, and mental, are invisible. And some disabled people are really good at passing as able-bodied. We do so for our own reasons—

reasons we don't need to, and shouldn't have to, explain to anyone.

But the accommodations model requires us to disclose our disabilities, it requires us to explain, to give up secrets we might not want to share. The accommodations model depends on invasions of privacy to work.

Accessibility, alternatively, means that a space is always, 100% of the time, welcoming to people with disabilities. Accessibility means that "accommodations" are integrated into a space and are not particularized to an individual—but rather created for our society as a whole. We, as a society, are disabled people. Therefore we, as a society, build spaces and procedures for disabled people.

It really is that simple.

Except it isn't. It isn't that simple because big, slow-moving structures such as federal government entities, state government entities, and workplaces, and professional organizations insist (incorrectly) that moving from an accommodation model to an accessibility model would be too expensive. So they put the burden on disabled *individuals*—the burden of cost, the burden of proof, the burden of just about everything that they, as the large, powerful entities, should be doing instead.

————

THERE IS one large entity that I've been a part of for years that tends to get the accessibility thing right. The Conference on College Composition and Communication (CCCC) is a professional organization in the humanities. It holds an annual conference that is attended by thousands of people. They meet in large cities, one that is often unfamiliar to most attendees. CCCC (pronounced "4-Cs") could run a clinic on how to make a conference accessible. Things aren't perfect, of course, in part because accessibility depends a lot on the attendees themselves (as I discuss later in this chapter). But for now, as an example, consider the accessibility guides the local committees put together. It is downloadable as a PDF from the conference website each year, and its link is located on the main conference webpage—not buried on some "disability accommodations" page.

The accessibility guide is incredible. No attendee—normate or disabled—has to ask how to get from the airport. The information is in there. No one has to ask what the accessible rooms, breezeways, or carpets are like. The creators of this document photograph them and describe them in detail. This is amazing work.

This is what accessibility looks like.

I really don't like that I'm amazed by this document. The reason I am amazed is because I so rarely encounter accessible material like this unless I'm attending a disability studies conference where, you know, they know how to get it right because disability is literally what they do.

I ATTENDED A RECENT CCCC CONFERENCE—I try to attend as frequently as I can. Before the conference, I spent time carefully preparing my talk. I prepared three things: a slide deck, a handout that was essentially a script of the presentation I intended to give, and a 2-page handout with other resources pertaining to my talk.

I then printed my slides and both handouts in large format, in a sans-serif, 18-point font. I printed 100% of my handouts in an accessible fashion—I didn't print any in small print. I then uploaded all of these materials to the conference website where they could be downloaded by anyone who might need them for accessibility purposes. When I delivered my talk, I provided a rich description of each slide in my deck. I included text of these rich descriptions on the script handout, too.

These are the steps that I take to ensure that all of my talks are accessible to anyone who comes to hear me, even when I don't anticipate anyone—at all—coming to hear me. (My talk was scheduled at 8am on a Friday. I wouldn't have come to hear me, either. The turnout was respectable, though, all things considered.)

When I prepare for a talk, I do not know whether anyone in my audience will have a hearing impairment. I do not know whether anyone in my audience will have a visual impairment. I do not know whether anyone in my audience will have any disability that will require my talk be accessible.

But, if it turns out my panel does have an audience, the likelihood that someone in the audience will have a disability is actually quite high. These days, one in five people in the United States is disabled, according the the U.S. Census Bureau. And because of the small amount of work that I have undertaken to make my talk accessible for everyone, no attendees in my audience will have to out themselves or their disabilities to ask for accommodations. For example, I will not ask this question: "Does anyone need a large-print handout"—because all of my handouts are large print.

Most importantly, disabled people in the audience will know that I anticipated their presence at my talk, that I wanted their presence at my talk.

I didn't just come up with this stuff out of my own head. *Composing Access* is a website hosted by The Ohio State University and authored by members of the Committee on Disability Issues in College Composition (a group that meets at the CCCC conference). The website that provides "various ideas for ways to enhance accessibility at conferences." There is, quite literally, no reason that anyone should be give inaccessible presentations any longer—not with the resources *Composing Access* provides. There's a great handout you can download for how to make your talk more accessible. There are videos. There are more resources than most conference-goers or organizers would ever need.

Creating an accessible talk for disabled audience members is a good enough reason for you to make your talk accessible. But an accessible talk isn't just good for disabled people. Here's what happens for normates when you make your talk accessible.

First, as the talk-giver, you make a better talk. Ask yourself, what's one of the worst things that can happen during a panel presentation? When a speaker goes too long. Wow, that is so annoying. It's annoying for the audience and for the other speakers. Literally no one likes it when someone goes too long. So—when you force yourself to write a script of your talk—even if you don't read your script—you force yourself to figure out everything you want to say in advance. And when you know what you want to say, you make a better talk. You don't end up with "Just one more point to make" and run over time. You can still speak extemporaneously, but you don't speak in tangents.

Second, as the talk-giver, you make a better slide deck. Have you ever forced yourself to write a description of your slides? Let me tell you, that exercise improves your slides *a lot*. Writing a verbal description of a visual slide forces you to have this conversation with yourself: "Wow, a typo. And do I really have six bullet points? Do I *need* six bullet points? Why did I pick such an ugly graphic?"

Third, when you give an accessible talk, you model accessibility to normates in the audience. Most conference attendees probably have no ideas about what the best practices are for preparing and delivering talks. If you deliver an accessible talk—and state at the outset that you are doing so—others can learn from you.

And then, when you do that, the one in five of us who have a disability don't have to ask for special accommodations. Instead, the conference will already be accessible for everyone.

———

An earlier version of this chapter first appeared on my blog at katieroseguestpryal.com on April 4 and 5, 2016.

1. Brittany Quinn, "TSA Agent Kruze: 'Was the surgery worth the pain?'" Medium.com, March 30, 2016.

BELIEVE YOUR COLLEAGUES WITH DISABILITIES

I n Chapter 6, I focused on accommodations for faculty and staff in higher education—how higher education institutions often fail to support their disabled workers. In their failure, institutions often place heavy burdens on their disabled workers—for example, the burden of jumping through excessive hoops in order to gain disability accommodations, or, the burden of hiding stigmatized disabilities lest workers suffer harassment.

Workers must force their institutions to comply with disability employment laws. This particular burden puts disabled workers in a double-bind: During the disability accommodations application process, a process grounded in suspicion toward disabled people, institutions require workers to reveal deeply personal medical information to prove that they deserve accommodations. Yet, in forcing disabled workers to disclose their private medical information, institutions put their workers at risk of ableism and stigma.

But individual faculty and staff can also create burdens for their disabled colleagues, often without realizing it. As I wrote in Chapter 8, as colleagues in academia, we should want to take responsibility for one another, and to support one another. Whether a colleague is helping an ill family member—a situation when most of us seem to have no problem reaching out and helping—or struggling to get disability accommodations at work, we all thrive better in conditions of mutual support.

I've encountered two main issues with collegial support for disabled workers in the academic workplace. On the one hand, not-so-good-natured people can be suspicious of a disabled colleague's need for accommodations. On the other hand, good-natured people can feel insecure about knowing how to help a disabled colleague. And because of this insecurity, they end up doing nothing at all.

This column addresses both of these issues: the suspicions, as well as the good-natured insecurity. My main message is this: even though you may have been taught otherwise, the best thing you can do is to believe your colleagues with disabilities. But because of how much suspicion is heaped on disabled people, setting aside those suspicions can be hard.

———

UNFOUNDED SUSPICIONS

All workplaces, including (and perhaps especially) academia, put a heavy burden on a disabled worker when it comes to getting disability accommodations. When I was in academia, even though I had a disability that would have warranted accommodations, I never sought them. And I never, ever would have. The invasion of privacy, the stigma, the fear of ableism—the general blowback that seeking accommodations would have brought—all of that would have been too high of a price to pay for the paltry accommodations my institution would have granted me.

Institutions seem to be so concerned that an employee might be faking a disability that they require mountains of invasive documentation. They require proof, heaps of proof, from people who are not the disabled person (such as doctors, occupational therapists, and more). Institutions won't accept, say, a sworn statement from a disabled person that she is, indeed, disabled.

They would never take a disabled employee's word for it. I often make this joke with my disabled friends: Can you even imagine being able to walk into a gatekeeper's office—such as a human resources department—and request accessibility based on your promise that you are disabled? And then, imagine this: You could just provide a description of your needs? And have the gatekeeper believe you and provide accommodations to meet your needs? Disabled people live in a world that, as a rule, doubts us. We must, every day, prove that our needs are real.

It's exhausting.

It doesn't help that the popular media creates even more suspicions by focusing on (usually mythic) abuse of disability accessibility—just take a look at the Anderson Cooper 60 Minutes segment on "Drive-By Lawsuits."[1] It begins by stating that "the Americans with Disabilities Act has thousands of very technical regulations, and this store [that Cooper is visiting] is in violation." When a writer wants to make a law sound unimportant, he calls it a "technicality." But to the people who rely on that law, those "technicalities" mean that we can live healthy, safe lives. They are—technically—serious.

————

BELIEVE YOUR COLLEAGUES

In this environment of suspicion, what can you do to help your disabled colleagues? The first thing you can do requires very little of you: you can believe your colleagues who have disabilities. You can set aside your suspicions. This might be hard at first because you have been trained to be suspicious of disabled people. We all have—that is the world we live in.

But you can make the radical decision that suspicion is not going to be your way of thinking any more.

Remember, the mountains of paperwork institutions require before granting any sort of accommodations are a manifestation of deep suspicion of disabled people. Institutions—and the government laws they act under—show mistrust of disabled people.

In this environment of suspicion, being a disabled staff or faculty member can feel incredibly isolating. You can help your colleague feel less isolated simply by being aware of, and believing, what she is going through.

Fight the urge to be suspicious. Believe your colleagues' disability stories. Despite the ways that the popular media can focus on abuse of the ADA, remember that those stories make the news because they are unusual. Most disabled people just want to be able to live our lives and do our jobs, just like everyone else.

———

An earlier version of this chapter first appeared as a column in *Women in Higher Education* on May 1, 2017.

1. "Action Alert: Anderson Cooper's ADA Attack on 60 Minutes," *The Advocacy Monitor*, Dec. 7, 2016.

PART III
TEACHING

HOW TO HAVE THE
ACCOMMODATIONS TALK

In Chapter 18, I describe how I worked to make my teaching universally accessible for all of my students, not just my students with disabilities. The impetus for the change in my teaching was a particular meeting with a disabled student. When she approached me, I asked her to tell me about what challenges she faced in the classroom. Given those challenges, I changed my teaching, and I found—to my surprise—that *all* of my students benefited from the changes. I'd stumbled upon universal design, in this particular case universal teaching design, that makes learning more accessible for everyone.

I'm briefly retelling this story as a preface to this chapter because this chapter is about the meeting that inspired my teaching changes in the first place—the meeting when my student approached me to request accommodations.

I'm very grateful to Past Katie for not ruining that student meeting. Over the years, I've since researched how to have these meetings better, since faculty and staff rarely receive training on how to meet with disabled students. (Did you receive training? I sure didn't.) Here are some tips for how to have the accommodations talk with your disabled students.

————

WHAT DO I DO FIRST WHEN A STUDENT APPROACHES ME TO REQUEST DISABILITY ACCOMMODATIONS?

First, smile. Smile even if you're not a smiler. Smile anyway. It's not about you—it's about your student. Next, say something like this: "I'm so glad you are sharing this information with me. I want to hear more." Your demeanor and your very first words will make the student feel that you aren't uncomfortable (which you won't be after you read this column), or worse, resentful. The best way to tank this meeting is to make an already-nervous student believe you don't want her to come to you.

A surprising number of faculty and staff are resentful when students approach them with disability accommodations requests. Because of this resentment, which these students have faced over and over—believe me, they have—students have developed defense mechanisms. These defense mechanisms might make a student seem, you know, defensive when she first approaches you. Rather than acting judgmental, or put off by the defensiveness, understand where this defensive emotion is coming from. The defensiveness is not about you—it's about every other time in this student's life when she was treated badly because of her disability.

Let's examine resentment and defensiveness more closely for a moment.

A student with a disability faces stigma. Stigma comes in a variety of forms. She might have to face the misperception that, because of her disability, she does not belong in higher education. She might have to face the misperception that her disability isn't real or that it isn't bad enough for accommodations. Or she might have to face the misperception that her disability is so bad that she can't succeed at all. Sometimes she has to face all of these misperceptions at the same time, putting her in a double bind—is her disability bad enough to warrant accommodations? And if her disability is actually so bad, shouldn't she just quit school? Sometimes the same person will say both of these things to her at once, forcing her to walk a disability tightrope.

When a student comes to you to have the accommodations talk, she doesn't know which of these beliefs you hold, or if you hold them all. So it is your job to reassure her that you believe her, and that you want to help her succeed in school.

———

DO I NEED TO PROTECT MY STUDENT'S PRIVACY?

Absolutely. The first thing you can do to show how much you respect your student's privacy is to offer a private place to talk. For instance, if a student approaches you after class about accommodations, offer an office space where you can speak privately. If a work-study student whom you supervise comes to you in a semi-public place, invite the student to a private conference room or to your office. Chances are the student is nervous about revealing her disability to you (for all of the reasons I discussed above), and offering privacy will help put her at ease.

Reassure her that you will continue to protect her privacy, both from other students and other faculty. Remember, students are not required to share their disability accommodation needs with faculty. She might have chosen to share her disability with you, but not with another professor. She might have chosen you because, for some reason, she trusts you. (That's a gift.) She might not feel that same level of trust with her other professors. Do not presume that she shared her disability with all of her professors. That means that, even if you know that she is in a class with a colleague of yours, you should not discuss her disability with that colleague.

Remember, as a faculty or staff member, you hold a position of power in this first meeting about accommodations. So take the initiative to tell the student that you will not discuss her disability. Tell her you will protect her privacy. Don't make her ask you to do so.

————

WHAT IF THE STUDENT'S DISABILITY IS ONE THAT I KNOW A LOT ABOUT?

Whatever you do, do not lecture the student on her own disability. I have had students come to me with the same disability that I have—literally the same diagnosis. And I have learned that the very best thing I can do is to keep my mouth shut and let my students teach me about their disabilities.

Let your student lead the conversation. Let her tell you what her needs are. Let her decide what, precisely, she needs to succeed in your class. Don't make those decisions for her. For example, don't insist that she sit in a certain place in the classroom or insist that she use a note-taker. She is in charge of what she needs regarding her accommodations. Don't force accommodations on her.

Work together to come up with a plan, one that you can work with and one that will meet the student's needs. If you work together in good faith, you will figure out a plan. If you find yourself stumped in trying to develop classroom or workplace accommodations, reach out to your on-campus student disability services office for ideas—they are professionals who do learning design for a living. You aren't alone in this.

WHAT IF IT SEEMS THAT MY STUDENT'S DISABILITY HAS CHANGED, DISAPPEARED, OR GOTTEN BETTER DURING THE SEMESTER?

All disabilities (both physical and psychiatric) can be changeable and unpredictable and inconsistent. Sometimes physical impairments require mobility aids, and sometimes they don't. We all have good days. Just because your student is having a good day or good week—or is appearing to—doesn't mean your student is faking needing a mobility aid. It means that when your student is able to walk unassisted, she wants to walk unassisted.

Whatever you do, resist the urge to be suspicious of your students with disabilities. Just resist. As I describe in so many chapters in this book (check out the prior two chapters, "Accessibility Is for Everyone" and "Believe Your Colleagues with Disabilities"), disabled people have dealt with the suspicions of normates their entire lives. The notion that a disabled person is lying is a cliché at this point.

Disabled people have been deemed untrustworthy by Western science, medicine, and law since time immemorial. That statement is not an exaggeration. In courtrooms, our memories are questioned on the witness stand. At the government level and the workplace level, the burden of proof for disability benefits is incredibly high. Don't become a cliché and mistrust your student because she seems to be having a week with more "spoons"—a disability community term used to describe the energy it takes to perform daily tasks. Try setting aside your suspicions and learn about spoons, instead.

To summarize: if you welcome your disabled student when she approaches you, offer her privacy and discretion, let her be the expert about her disability, use campus services when you need help teaching with her disability, and believe her story about her disability (both at the beginning and throughout your relationship), you are well on the way to being a strong advocate for students with disabilities.

―――――

An earlier version of this chapter first appeared as a column in *Women in Higher Education* on June 1, 2017. I wrote this column in response to an essay in *The Chronicle of Higher Education* by Gail A. Hornstein, "Why I Dread the Accommodations Talk," published on March 26, 2017.

TRIGGER WARNINGS ARE A DISABILITY ISSUE

Last fall, I went to see a screening of *The Hunting Ground*, a documentary about campus sexual assault, when it came to Chapel Hill where I live. About halfway through the film, my heart started racing, I started shaking, and I realized I was crying. I dashed from the theater and went to the bathroom to splash water on my face, and then I went to the coffee shop next door to settle down with tea. After about forty-five minutes, I returned to the theater but stood near the door, so that I could leave periodically to take breaks.

As a rape survivor, I had a totally normal post-traumatic reaction to a movie about rape. It took me another two viewings to make it through the entire movie. I didn't mind the emotional work it took.

In fact, I expected it: Before the screening, two people who helped make the documentary provided a trigger warning to the audience. They reassured us, stating that there was no shame in walking out if we needed to.

Being warned in advance that I would possibly (even likely) experience the documentary as a triggering event helped me prepare for such a traumatic reaction, recognize it when it was happening, take care of myself—including forgiving myself—and return to the film prepared to continue learning from it.

———

TRIGGER WARNINGS MISUNDERSTOOD AS CODDLING

These days, there is a strong debate around the term "trigger warnings." Much of the debate centers around academics and whether teachers should provide trigger warnings (also called "content warnings") for students. Academics seem to either value trigger warnings or abhor them.

The debate over trigger warnings has gone beyond the small blurbs of text on syllabi or assignment sheets and into discussions of whether college students today are coddled infants incapable of facing emotional challenges.

What seems to be missing from the debate is how much trigger warnings are not about coddling, but rather about disability. An anxiety reaction, a post-traumatic reaction, or any other reaction to material (e.g., text, film, music) that causes an involuntary response in your brain and body *is a disability issue.*

As disability studies scholar and professor Margaret Price wrote in her letter to *The New Yorker*, "Trigger warnings serve to prevent panic attacks or flashbacks that impede one's ability to engage in discussion. ... They are intended to enable everyone to remain present and alert enough to be challenged and discomfited."[1] Contrary to the notion of protecting students from challenging material, trigger warnings, like the one I received before watching *The Hunting Ground*, can help students with disabilities participate fully.

But opponents of trigger warnings prefer the "coddled children" red herring (along with the "academic freedom" red herring) to an understanding of trigger warnings as an accessibility measure. Indeed, you don't need to read much past the *New York Times* headline in its lead piece by Jennifer Medina on the subject to get this impression: "Warning: The Literary Canon Could Make Students Squirm."[2] Lisa Hajjar, a professor of sociology at the University of California, Santa Barbara, was interviewed for the *Times* piece—at the time, UCSB was considering a campus-wide trigger warning policy. Hajjar called trigger warnings "inimical to academic freedom." Furthermore, "The presumption there is [sic] that students should not be forced to deal with something that makes them uncomfortable is absurd or even dangerous." Her solution to in-class post-traumatic reactions is to point out that "[a]ny student can request some sort of individual accommodation."

Besides revealing her misunderstanding of the nature of trigger warnings (how exactly do they limit academic freedom?) and her underestimation of her students (how would they be able to avoid discomfort and why would they want to?), Hajjar's words also reveal the underlying disability-rights nature of the trigger warning debate. She casually tosses out the term "individual accommodation" as a viable solution. By suggesting that her students seek "individual accommodation," she implicitly recognizes (1) some of her students have disabilities and (2) her class creates a disabling environment for those students.

This professor's solution to put the onus on students to seek "individual accommodation" through what I'm presuming is the student disability office reveals not only a lack of empathy on the professor's part but also a lack of understanding of disabling environments and what we can do to correct them. But first, we have to understand what it means to be triggered in the first place.

———

HOW TRIGGERS WORK

Angela M. Carter, in "Teaching with Trauma: Trigger Warnings, Feminism, and Disability Pedagogy," helpfully draws the distinction between being triggered and being merely challenged in class: "To be triggered is to mentally and physically re-experience a past trauma in such an embodied manner that one's affective response literally takes over the ability to be present in one's bodymind."[3]

Carter's words are reminiscent of Price's letter to *The New Yorker* and her description of panic attacks and flashbacks as impediments to class participation. Carter writes: "When this [triggering] occurs, the triggered individuals often feel a complete loss of control and disassociation from the bodymind. This is not a state of injury, but rather a state of disability."

For many students with disabilities of this sort, getting accommodations is not easy. First of all, students seeking accommodations for psychiatric disabilities are more often met with skepticism than those seeking accommodations for physical disabilities. This skepticism has to do with disability service offices gatekeeping accommodations because they believe students will use such accommodations to cheat and because of the stigma still attached to psychiatric disability. Furthermore, due to this stigma, many students are afraid to seek accommodations, leaving a paper trail of their disability.

Which leads me to wonder: Do professors who insist that students create a paper trail of their stigmatized disabilities so that such professors can take a stand against trigger warnings on their syllabi need to reconsider their priorities as teachers and mentors?

Rather than insisting on "individualized accommodations" so that you can create a disabling environment in your classroom, take an accessibility approach and allow all students to participate fully.

———

An earlier version of this chapter first appeared as a column in *Women in Higher Education* on March 1, 2016.

1. Margaret Price, "Literary Warnings," The Mail, *The New Yorker*, June 30, 2014.
2. Jennifer Medina, "Warning: The Literary Canon

Could Make Students Squirm," *The New York Times*, May 17, 2014.

3. Angela M. Carter, "Teaching with Trauma: Trigger Warnings, Feminism, and Disability Pedagogy," *Disability Studies Quarterly*, 2015, Volume 35, Issue 2.

HOW MAKING MY TEACHING ACCESSIBLE MADE MY TEACHING BETTER

Disability studies was my field of research for nearly a decade. But it wasn't until I had a visually impaired student in my classroom that I learned to make my teaching truly accessible. And the remarkable outcome of the accessibility changes I made to my teaching was this: making my teaching accessible made my teaching better—for all of my students.

———

ACCESSIBILITY VS. ACCOMMODATION

As a teacher, it can be easy to feel put-upon to have to accommodate the needs of a student with a disability. You have your way of teaching, and it works for you. You're good at your job. Then, suddenly, a student shows up who is hearing impaired, visually impaired, cognitively impaired, or what have you, and suddenly, you must accommodate that student's impairment.

At least, that's what it seems like from the outside.

In reality, you have students with disabilities in your classes all the time. Many students elect not to seek official accommodations. Many students do seek accommodations through student services, but they elect not to tell their professors out of fear of engendering bad feelings. Contrary to the "special-snowflake" theory of "the kids these days," it's unusual for a student with a disability to want special treatment. They just want to be able to get by like everyone else.

The difference between "special treatment" and getting by like everyone else is the difference between "accommodations" and "accessibility." As I explained in other chapters, "accommodation" shifts the burden to the disabled person. Accommodation requires a disabled person to interact with gatekeepers, to ask for something extra, and to prove that she deserves accommodation in the first place—that she is "disabled enough." The very word, "accommodate," implies that the world is doing a favor for the disabled student—or worse, doing something required by mandate.

"Accessibility" is entirely different from accommodation. As I've explained, it means that accommodations are already integrated into a space and are not particularized to an individual. Rather, in an accessible classroom or space, accommodations are built in, built out, and ready for all people. Accessibility should be our goal as teachers, *not* accommodation. Accessibility requires a change in mindset— and a change in teaching tactics.

The goal, in our courses, is what is called "Universal Design." The North Carolina State University Center for Universal Design has great resources on the topic. Universal design, according to the concept's founder Ron Mace, "is the design of products and environments to be usable by all people, to the greatest extent possible, without the need for adaptation or specialized design."

Universal design is the goal of accessibility. As NCSU's Center explains, "Universal design benefits people of all ages and abilities"—not just people with disabilities, although it benefits them, too.

HOW MY TEACHING CHANGED—FOR THE BETTER

After my visually impaired student let me know about her disability, I asked her to tell me what sorts of things I could do to help her have a better experience in my class. For a moment, she stood there in silence. Apparently, professors rarely asked her for her wish list.

She told me that because she couldn't see the whiteboard, describing what I was writing on it would be helpful. Even better: having access to my lecture notes. She would need handouts in PDF form rather than printed out on paper, and ideally in advance of class, so she could read them using her laptop.

These requests seemed so imminently reasonable to me. And they also got me thinking about ways I could integrate her requests into my teaching. I mean, wouldn't everyone do better if they could read the handouts before class? Wouldn't everyone prefer to have a PDF copy they could access whenever they needed to, rather than having to keep up with a paper copy?

I considered her whiteboard request. What happens to all of that information that I sketch on the whiteboard during class? In the past, I'd had more than one student come up with a cell phone to photograph the board to reference later, preserving the graphical representation of our class discussion. I wondered, was there an alternative to the whiteboard that would allow for our class discussions to happen in real time, but still be preserved afterward in a more useful fashion than a photograph? Better yet, could this alternative be accessible?

A UNIVERSAL DESIGN ALTERNATIVE TO THE WHITEBOARD

The first day of class, I projected a blank document from my laptop onto the room's projection screen. At the top of the document, I typed the class meeting date and the name of the class. I told the class that this document would be our "Class Record." I told them that for the rest of the semester, at the end of each class meeting, I would review the class record for errors and completeness, and then post it as a PDF to our course management system for all to have.

Our class discussion began, and I began to type. I couldn't draw diagrams, so I had to get more creative with my use of words. Also, it was hard at first, typing while running a class discussion. But it wasn't any harder than learning how to write on a blackboard or whiteboard. Honestly, after a few classes, it got easy. After all, I don't have to look at the keyboard to type.

And my students really got into it. "Put that on the class record!" they would request during class, when I said something they found particularly helpful. They would take their own notes, and then supplement those notes with the record.

I started using the record to prepare my lectures. On the class record, I would type up an outline of the class that I'd prepared in advance, and then fill in the blanks as we went through discussion. And at the end of every class, I'd review, fix typos, explain a few things that needed further information, and then post the PDF. And if I forgot to post that PDF, I'd receive no fewer than five emails from students politely requesting I do so. In short, all of my students loved the class record.

Better still, the class record cut way down on follow-up questions. Students knew to check the class record first. Most of the time, a question about class was answered in the record. Students who missed class knew they needed to get notes from classmates and download the class record. In the end, the class record actually decreased my workload as a teacher.

I'd made the ephemeral, messy whiteboard into a readable, accessible, reproducible document, and all of my students benefited—including the ones with disabilities who'd never told me about their disabilities and never will. After that semester, the class record became an integral part of my teaching.

That's accessibility—integrating the needs of all students into your teaching, including the students whose disabilities you will never know about.

———

An earlier version of this chapter first appeared as a column in *Women in Higher Education* on March 1, 2017.

WHAT DO PSYCHIATRICALLY DISABLED FACULTY OWE OUR STUDENTS?

Back in 2014, when I first I (albeit only vaguely) starting disclosing my own psychiatric disability in a series of columns for *Chronicle Vitae*, I received many emails from people seeking my guidance with their own challenges with disabilities in the workplace. I tried to answer every one. I felt the strong pull of moral duty—to let people who reached out to me (usually in secret) know that they were not alone, that someone was looking out for them, even from afar. Sometimes there was not much I could do, but I could answer the emails.

I had to. After all, many of these people wouldn't be emailing me if they had anyone else to turn to.

Some of you know that "have to" feeling. Students and junior faculty come to you for mentoring, even though you are not technically their adviser, because they have nowhere else to go, or because they believe that you—and perhaps only you—could possibly understand what they are going through. Those hours of unpaid, underappreciated mentoring service are what I (and others) call "bonus" work.

Research has confirmed what many women and professors of color already knew: We spend more time doing bonus work in the academy than our white, male counterparts. I'm talking about the unpaid advising work that certain members of the academy are expected to perform because of who they are. But the problem is, that service doesn't count for much, if anything, when it comes time for promotion, raises, retention, hiring, or (if one is so lucky) tenure.

For example, women spend more time on mentoring. Students are more likely to approach a female faculty member for advice—especially when they are in emotional distress—because, statistically speaking, as Bachen et al. have shown, students perceive female faculty members to be more nurturing.[1]

Students of color turn to faculty of similar racial and ethnic backgrounds because these students tend to find a sympathetic ear to the unique challenges that they face. Yet mentors of color can be rare. Therefore, in fields where there are few women and people of color—of the nearly seventy faculty members in my division, only two are African-American women—the bonus work of mentoring becomes an even heavier burden.

If we say yes to every student who comes through our office doors, we necessarily have less time for our own work. If we say no to them, then students—and, surprisingly (or not?), our colleagues—consider us selfish. Plus, we might think we're selfish.

That double-bind has been well documented. Professor Debra A. Harley titled her research on the heavy service burden borne by black women faculty at predominantly white institutions "Maids of Academe."[2] Joya Misra and her coauthors called the "service gap" that holds women back from achieving higher levels of professional success in academia the "Ivory Ceiling."[3]

Professor of English Katie Hogan has some great recommendations for women and professors of color on "managing" our "service duties," which include refusing to "idealize service" and keeping a "service log."[4] Another solution is for all of us to recognize that mentoring is hard work that can be hired—and paid for—outside of an academic department, as Kerry Ann Rockquemore has observed.[5]

Until the service gap is closed, it will remain a problem for all underrepresented faculty (who will be sought as mentors) and junior faculty and students (who will need mentors) in the academy.

THE DISABILITY SERVICE GAP

Professors with disabilities are underrepresented in the academy, in part because, as Stephanie L. Kerschbaum and Margaret Price write, they often have "concerns about how they may be perceived as a consequence of disclosing a disability," and therefore choose not to disclose.[6]

Some professors believe faculty should disclose their own

disabilities in order to better help students with disabilities. Professor of English Linda Kornasky has an invisible disability—unilateral hearing impairment—and she has urged academics with invisible disabilities (more than once) to "come out" to their students and colleagues.[7] She writes that there are "unique benefits [to] students with disabilities" if they can have "mentors with disabilities."

I am not here to dispute Kornasky's claim. She describes the occasion when she first told a class about her disability. After class, a student came to her and disclosed his own hearing disability—and then asked to be Kornasky's advisee. Indeed, she writes, "In the decade after that first disclosure, dozens of students, some with hearing impairments and others with a range of visible and invisible disabilities, have followed this young man, confidently informing me that they too are disabled and seeking me out for mentoring." I'm glad her students had a mentor whom they could relate to. And I'm glad that Kornasky felt energized enough to do this bonus work.

But in a world where bonus work remains underpaid and under-recognized, should we be advocating that professors—especially if they are contingent ones, who are already underpaid and under-recognized—take on this bonus work for free?

———

MENTORING WITH A PSYCHIATRIC DISABILITY

The question of who should do bonus work grows even more complex when we're talking about professors with psychiatric disabilities mentoring students with the same.

Law professor Brian Clarke insists that faculty must "come out" with their psychiatric disabilities because students "need to see that suffering from depression or anxiety or bipolar disorder will not curse them for all time and destroy their lives. ... They need us to be brave and be honest."[8]

If a professor takes Kornasky's and Clarke's advice and decides to disclose an invisible psychiatric disability, not only must the professor contend with potential stigma and ableism, but also with a new challenge: the bonus work of being the go-to person on campus for students with psychiatric disabilities.

As Kornasky describes, students with disabilities will often seek a mentor who understands the challenges of living with similar disabilities. Professor of Social Work Ruth C. White described just this phenomenon to me when I interviewed her. White is, in her words, an "immigrant black woman who identifies with the queer community." After she began her career as a professor, she publicly disclosed her bipolar disorder. Although she was concerned that students would question her "competence," the opposite came to pass. In her student evaluations, she told me, "I get positive feedback about my 'normalization' of mental illness." Furthermore, she has taken on a mentoring role for students with psychiatric disabilities who "feel safe to come to [her] when they are having a hard time."

When Drexel law professor Lisa McElroy (now Tucker)

first disclosed her anxiety disorder on *Slate*,[9] she told me she spent three days straight answering emails from students and other people across the country who had similar disabilities. She has spent countless hours since then mentoring people who had no one else to turn to.

Like Tucker, I, too, worked in a law school. Estimates put law students at a particularly high risk for depression and anxiety (around 40% according to one study). As far as I know, no faculty members in my department are open about their psychiatric disabilities, but chances are, there were others besides me who had them. One thing I am certain about: when students come to you suffering with a psychiatric disability, and you have experienced a similar kind of suffering, it is really hard to turn them away.

Even when I was first writing this chapter as a column for *Chronicle Vitae*, I feared that students and others reading it would soon hesitate to come to me out of fear of being a bother to me. The last thing I wanted was to discourage people from seeking my help.

Because students and junior faculty with psychiatric disabilities need mentoring. But those of us who do this bonus mentoring work get taxed for doing it. For everyone's sake, this bonus work tax is a structural problem that administrators who possess far more power than I do must fix.

We want to help, yet too often we end up paying a price. In the words of Jay Dolmage (on Twitter), a professor of disability studies at the University of Waterloo, the bonus work is "an obligation, a trap, an honour, a burden, a 'gift,' and on and on."

An earlier version of this chapter first appeared as a column in *Chronicle Vitae* on August 28, 2014.

1. Christine M. Bachen et al., "Assessing the Role of Gender in College Students' Evaluations of Faculty," *Communication Education*, 1999, Volume 48, Issue 3, Pages 193-210. dx.doi.org/10.1080/03634529909379169.

2. Debra A. Harley, "Maids of Academe: African American Women Faculty at Predominately White Institutions," *Journal of African American Studies*, March 2008, Volume 12, Issue 1, Pages 19–36.

3. Joya Misra et al., "The Ivory Ceiling of Service Work," *Academe*, Jan. 2011.

4. Katie Hogan, "Managing Service Duties," *Inside Higher Ed*, Jan. 8, 2010.

5. Kerry Ann Rockquemore, "Mentoring Is a Business. Don't Fear It." *Chronicle Vitae*, May 14, 2014.

6. Stephanie L. Kerschbaum and Margaret Price, "Perils and Prospects of Disclosing Disability Identity in Higher Education," *Diversity US Blog*, March 3, 2014.

7. Linda Kornasky, "Identity Politics and Invisible Disability in the Classroom," *Inside Higher Education*, March 17, 2009.

8. Brian Clarke, "Law Professors, Law Students and

Depression: A Story of Coming Out," *The Faculty Lounge*, March 31, 2014.

9. Lisa T. McElroy (now Tucker), "Worrying Enormously About Small Things," *Slate*, July 18, 2013.

WE ARE NOT PREPARED FOR STUDENTS IN DISTRESS

W hen your students break down in tears in your office and share their anguish, how are you supposed to respond?

Most faculty aren't trained to deal with students experiencing emotional distress, so befuddlement is an understandable reaction, as DrMellivora (a blogging pen name) noted on *Tenure, She Wrote*, in a post titled "I'm Your Professor, Not Your Therapist!"[1] DrMellivora wondered what you should do for a weeping student: "Politely ignore? Offer Kleenex? Ask details?" When students shared their more serious psychiatric crises with her, she felt, rightfully, unprepared: "Should I have reached out sooner, to find out why he wasn't turning assignments in? This doesn't really seem like something you should learn through trial and error!"

"It's kind of sad," DrMellivora wrote, "that I spent so many years preparing for the mechanics of a position like this, and yet have no idea what to do in these emotional situations that have the potential to have real, long-term impacts on students." She's a good educator, and she's concerned.

Her confusion about how to react in these situations is not unusual. After all, professors in fields outside of psychiatric caregiving are not trained to give psychiatric care. Why *should* she have known what to do? As the title to her post suggests, this work is not her job.

But as educators, we are on the front lines of students' mental-health issues, and we are often called upon, in the heat of the moment, to listen to what may be shocking revelations from our students—about their mental health, addiction, trauma, or more. And if you are a graduate teaching assistant or an adjunct, often teaching lower-level classes and small sections, you are more likely to receive such revelations, as you might be the only instructor who knows a student's name.

These days, our students appear to be even more at risk of mental-health crises. A recent study by researchers at the University of California at Los Angeles found that nearly 10 percent of college freshmen in 2013 reported feeling depressed "frequently," compared with 2009, when only 6.1 percent did. The consequence, according to the research, is "that students with lower levels of emotional health wind up being less satisfied with college and struggle to develop a sense of belonging on campus, even after four years of college." Given the high likelihood that you will encounter a student in distress, and that you aren't a trained expert in counseling, what should you do?

I interviewed Ruth Ann McKinney, who is trained in both law and counseling, and is a clinical professor of law emeritus and a former assistant dean at the University of North Carolina School of Law. For years, she directed the Academic Success program at the law school, which provided support to students in distress. Here is her advice.

————

BE GENTLE WITH YOURSELF

McKinney recognizes that faculty members are often unprepared to deal with the surprise of a student in distress. For academics, being unprepared can feel unsettling. We just don't like it, in part because we aren't used to it. "Often, as faculty members," she said, "we are geared toward interacting with students on an intellectual basis. We are eager and ready for a cognitive discussion of the subject matter of our courses. But when a student expresses strong emotions of any kind in our office, it often catches us off guard." And being caught off guard can make us even less willing to listen: "Few people like to be surprised in any social interaction, and being surprised by a student who becomes emotional (veering away from the cognitive, which we more often expect) is no exception. It is, at best, disconcerting. At worst, it can be alarming."

Although you should ensure that a student leaves your office safely, you can set boundaries. "As an adult in the student's environment, and as a concerned educator," McKinney said, "you probably have a moral responsibility to assess how big a crisis the student is in and to make sure that the student is safe." But ensuring a student's safety does not require that you sacrifice your own mental health: "You don't have to solve the student's problems, and you don't have to be the only one who gets in on the discussion. Also, you don't ever have to pursue a conversation that you are not comfortable pursuing."

Indeed, McKinney said, it is OK if "you are a person who is not comfortable with other people's feelings, or if you don't have time to deal with an emotional situation right now." You just need to communicate that to the student: "Tell the student that in as nonjudgmental and kind a way as you can."

McKinney provided some perfectly acceptable language you might use in this case. Say something like, "I can see that you are in a very tough situation and I appreciate your sharing your feelings with me. It is understandable that you are upset. I am not very good at handling strong feelings, but I know someone who would be a better listener than me. I'm going to give [that person] a call now and see if we can walk down to his office together."

Be gentle with yourself. If you are thrown by a student's outburst or emotional outpour, that is OK. Everyone has different strengths. Don't beat yourself up. Just know who to ask for help. Which leads us to her next piece of advice.

————

KNOW WHOM TO ASK FOR HELP

"Every wise educator should anticipate that, at some point, he or she will have a student who is emotionally distraught in the educator's office," McKinney said. "The smart thing to do is to have a strategy in place for situations that go beyond what you know your tolerance for emotional discussions to be." If you know that your tolerance is low, you need to have some numbers on your office speed dial.

Before the semester starts, McKinney suggests, figure out who that contact should be. Then, "drop by that person's office and introduce (or reintroduce) yourself and confirm how that person would like you to handle a situation involving a student who is upset in your office." That way you have plans in place when an emergency arises, and don't have to come up with something on the fly.

Furthermore, you need to know just when to dial that number. "We teach people, not automatons," McKinney said. "People have emotions. As educators, we are sometimes in a position to help students grow in healthy ways at a crossroads in their lives." However, she added: "We are not therapists, we are not the police, we are not family, and we need to recognize our limitations." When you hit your limits, use that phone number.

————

MIND THE RED FLAGS

Red flag moments are the ones where you definitely need to ask for help. McKinney listed some of the most important ones to watch out for:

Psychological distress: "Do not try to make a psychological assessment if a situation looks remotely odd to you. Instead, tell the student you care about him or her enough to make sure he or she gets the help needed to find happiness. Then make the referral you rehearsed ahead of time to the right person in your educational environment."

Confidentiality: "Do not get lured into promising confidentiality from the get-go. If a student says, 'May I tell you something in confidence?' Respond (immediately, and warmly and kindly): 'It sounds like you have something important on your mind. I would be honored to listen (that is, only if you would be; but if you're not a good listener, say so at this point and refer the student to someone who is), but I can't promise confidentiality. If what you tell me puts you or someone else in danger, then out of concern for you, we will need to involve someone who can help.'"

Isolation: "Do not get involved in emotional discussions alone with a student at a time when your building is not well occupied. Instead, make the referral quickly and early, or ask the student to come back tomorrow."

Suicide: "Do not be afraid to ask the suicide question. If a student seems extraordinarily upset or depressed, you can and should ask, 'You sound overwhelmed and exhausted. Have you had thoughts about suicide?' You will not put the idea in the student's head. Most (but not all) suicidal individuals will answer honestly. Also, follow your instincts. If you remain concerned, make the referral in a genuine and compassionate way."

Most important, McKinney notes, "Do not make a student feel guilty or inadequate for having showed emotions in your office. We are all human."

———

An earlier version of this chapter first appeared as a column in *Chronicle Vitae* on Oct. 2, 2015.

1. DrMellivora, "I'm your professor, not your therapist!," *Tenure, She Wrote*, Nov. 11, 2013, retrieved from tenureshewrote.wordpress.com/2013/11/11/im-your-professor-not-your-therapist/.

THE SECRET LIFE OF THE GRADUATE
STUDENT

When I was in graduate school, my fellow students and I worked hard on our studies. We worked hard to earn our graduate stipends, teaching three or more courses a year. Many of us also worked extra jobs to make ends meet—at Starbucks, law firms, used book stores, and more. Many of us partied like it was 1999. (It was not, in fact, 1999. It was the early aughts.)

Now and then, some of us struggled personally—with addiction, mental illness, cognitive issues, major health crises and tragedies, and domestic violence.

We kept these struggles among ourselves. We didn't want our professors and advisers to know about our less-than-perfect private lives. We didn't want them to know if a fellow student were drinking too much or struggling with a bad relationship. Instead, we graduate students huddled together and helped each other privately. We didn't want to risk hurting a fellow graduate student's reputation in the department.

Because that's what was at stake: our reputations. We put on our professional masks for seminars, teaching, and meetings with advisers. And we kept up a barrier, for as long as we could, between what we knew was going on among "us" and what "they" would know about it. We believed "they," for the most part, didn't want to know.

We were living a secret life about which our professors knew very little.

———

WHY A SECRET LIFE?

Most professors have a vision of how an ideal graduate student performs. When I was in graduate school, some professors even told us, in great detail, descriptions of their ideal. Some of us believed that if we deviated from that ideal, we would have trouble getting funding, securing recommendations, or finding jobs. We were often proven right: With few exceptions, the closer we tracked the ideal, the more we were rewarded.

Likewise, we believed that if a friend deviated from the ideal, it was our duty to help that friend get back on track. We circled the proverbial wagons and helped each other as best we could. Help included giving a woman who'd lost her home to an unstable partner a place to sleep—and keeping her secret from faculty who might see her as an unstable victim if they found out. It included helping a friend with his seminar papers when he was having cognitive difficulties. In retrospect—knowing what I know now about disability—his cognitive difficulties would likely have been aided by disability services had he sought those accommodations. But seeking accommodations when you aren't an undergraduate can be rough, indeed.

After teaching at the graduate level for many years, I realize that faculty, for the most part, aren't equipped to know about graduate students' struggles. Put simply, most professors are not prepared to aid students in distress (as I write about in the previous chapter). If indeed it's true that graduate students in the United States (and elsewhere) are struggling with mental health and addiction issues at high rates—and it appears that it is—then we need to rethink whether graduate schools have a duty to accept the full person, the nonideal, and whether departments are inadvertently creating disabling environments in which graduate students feel forced to hide their struggles, to everyone's detriment.

A PROFESSOR'S POINT OF VIEW

I interviewed a fellow professor to seek another viewpoint on this issue. Maggie (a pseudonym), a humanities professor at a large research university, works in a department with many graduate students. She directs dissertations and sits on dissertation committees—the total number of graduate students whose work she closely advises hovers in the double-digits. Indeed, I selected her as an interview subject because of her close involvement with a large number of graduate students.

I asked her first about whether she received training—either in graduate school or on the job—in how to help graduate students who are struggling with personal crises. She replied, "There is little to no training that focuses on graduate students in particular, either in graduate school or as part of professional development for faculty." She noted, "Most faculty, I'd say, don't really know what to do or how to handle students in distress."

Furthermore, in her department, graduate students tend to keep their struggles secret from faculty until the secrets can't be kept any longer: "In my department, we often only find out about these kinds of issues when it reaches a crisis point." She described one incident in which a faculty member "found out that a graduate student hadn't been attending any classes for ... weeks," and "didn't respond to phone calls or emails." Only after someone actually went to the student's apartment did the professor realize that the student was dealing with severe depression and had dropped out of the program. The department "could have maybe helped the student and the student might still be enrolled," she said, had the department known of the student's struggles earlier.

What Maggie describes is similar to my own memories from graduate school. We all tried to handle problems privately until they grew too big for us to handle anymore. Sometimes—similar to the situation in Maggie's department—our fear of reprisals had terrible consequences.

Maggie gave another example: Upon finding "out that a student had been staying in his office ... instead of going back to his apartment because he was afraid of harming himself," faculty took him to the local hospital and perhaps saved his life.

"This was another case where faculty only found out when it had reached a crisis point." Basically, Maggie said, "I don't think faculty have a good sense of what their graduate students are going through unless it reaches one of these boiling points."

BREAK THE SILENCE

How can faculty help break down barriers of communication to encourage students to come forward? How can we encourage communication before a crisis becomes a crisis? After all, as Maggie pointed out, "At least in my experience, the majority of faculty would want to know about issues affecting their students' lives and would be willing to help. They just don't always find out about what is going on until things have gotten very serious."

So what can faculty do to help students understand it's OK to come forward?

First, show students that you're willing to help. At a basic level, for example, put a sign on your office door—"I'm a friend of neurodiversity"—that indicates your openness to discussing unconventional struggles. Then see what happens. Students with depression, bipolar disorder, anxiety disorder, and more might, with luck, decide that they can trust you with their secrets. You don't have to be an expert to help students in distress. You just have to be willing to listen and know whom to call for help.

Second, during orientation, have faculty and senior

graduate students talk openly about collaboration in personal—
not just professional—challenges. From Day One, establish a
culture in which these struggles are shared among faculty, staff,
and students. Build trust by promising students that they won't
be penalized for failing to meet some fictional "ideal" model of a
graduate student. And then, most importantly, keep that
promise.

———

An earlier version of this chapter first appeared as a column in
Chronicle Vitae on May 19, 2016.

PART IV
BEYOND THE ACADEMY

A MOTHER'S SUICIDE ATTEMPT AND
THE GUILTY BURDEN OF STATISTICS

WHAT DOES IT MEAN TO HAVE A CRAZY MOM?

In the February 2015 issue of *JAMA Psychiatry*, researchers published their findings from an extraordinary longitudinal study.[1] "Familial Pathways to Early-Onset Suicide Attempt: A 5.6-Year Prospective Study" followed 701 children of 334 parents who had attempted suicide. This study is unique in both its scope and its duration. Its findings show that having a parent who attempted suicide, even controlling for other factors, "conveys a nearly 5-fold increased odds of suicide attempt in offspring."

You might not see it if you aren't looking for it, but one of the subtexts of this study is motherhood, along with its favorite hobgoblin, guilt.

Toward the end of the article, the researchers talk about the possible weaknesses of their study. One weakness was this:

"Probands are mostly female, so we lack the power to detect whether the effect of maternal suicide attempt is greater than the effect of paternal suicide attempt, as is suggested by some studies."

A proband, for non-geneticists out there, is a starting point for a genetic study. In this study, a proband is a parent. But, as the researchers note, most of their probands were mothers. The researchers are saying that the majority of the parents in this study were moms who tried to kill themselves. They're also saying that results of other similar studies show that, when compared to dads, moms attempting suicide have a greater influence on whether their children attempt suicide.

OK.

Say you're a mom. You've just clawed yourself out of a debilitating depression. Indeed, you only barely survived, because you actually attempted suicide (once, maybe twice). You are so overjoyed to be able to appreciate your family again, to feel happiness again. But now that you're back on your feet—literally—you come across a study that tells you that your suicide attempt might have fucking cursed your children.

Man, you thought the guilt from not being able to breastfeed your second kid because of your postpartum depression was bad. But that guilt has nothing on the guilt you feel now.

You think of mythic curses throughout history. Of Oedipus and the house of Cadmus. Of Moses and his plagues. Of Jezebel cursing Elijah.

Then you look at your sons.

———

WHAT DOES IT MEAN TO HAVE A CRAZY MOM?

Naturally, the study suggests interventions for preventing suicide in "offspring." "Offspring." So clinical. So unlike the little-limbed bodies that sprite around your house and yard, leaving contrails of life in their wake.

One intervention, of course, is better parenting. "Impulsive aggression was an important precursor of mood disorder and could be targeted in interventions designed to prevent youth at high familial risk from making a suicide attempt." But in order to intervene and treat impulsive aggression, you'd have to pick up on the behavior in the first place.

Guess whose job it is to notice behavioral changes in their kids and ensure such medical interventions occur? Mostly moms. We make most medical decisions for our children—that's why we get blamed for anti-vaxxing.

According to the Kaiser Family Foundation, who researched gender roles in medical decision-making, "In most households, women are the managers of their families' health." Only 20% of fathers select a children's doctor. Only 16% of fathers take children to their doctor's appointments. Only 20% make sure children receive the care the doctors recommend. And only three fucking percent actually take care of a sick child, compared to 39% of women—with the rest falling on "joint responsibility" or a third party.

So, you've just survived depression. You survived a suicide attempt (or, let's be honest, a couple). You have new rituals, new medicines, new doctor's appointments—all for you, to ensure your health. To ensure that you can be a good mom.

But now you're feeling some pressure to make sure your kids make it through their teen years alive.

———

WHAT DOES IT MEAN TO HAVE A CRAZY MOM?

According to the latest scientific research, having a crazy mom means my kids are five times more likely to attempt suicide than kids who don't have a crazy mom.

I came across the JAMA Psychiatry study as I was ripping through the psychiatric and neuro newswires, part of my job as a reporter of mental health issues. Whenever a new study is particularly newsworthy, I read it and write about it. This study on early-onset suicide caught my eye because of its sheer scope. So many people studied over so many years.

But as I read this study, my work got personal—because most of the parents who attempted to kill themselves were the children's moms. In other words, the study was the most epic Crazy Mom study ever conducted. And it was published in February of 2015, just months after I kissed my children good-bye, dressed in dark clothes, and walked into traffic to die.

Hey guys, not sure if you're still collecting probands with offspring, but I got one for you right here.

The night I planned my death, I knew, to a certainty beyond any doubt (empirical, reasonable, or otherwise), that my children would be better off with a new and better mother, my husband with a new and better wife.

That's a thing I did that will never undo itself. The tricky thoughts that led to the thing I did, those thoughts that chased me for weeks and weeks until they had me convinced (and I'm a very skeptical person), those thoughts will always be there as memories. They had marvelous suggestions, too. Pills. Car wrecks. Pills and car wrecks.

I can't even guarantee that those thoughts won't come back. I just have a better plan this time.

But here's the thing. I'm a proband now. One with offspring. It doesn't matter what I do. I've cursed them already. It's too late.

So I watch my children closely for any signs of emotional expression beyond the normal, that might represent impulsive aggression, even though they're likely too young to even be expressing these kinds of emotions in the first place.

I mean whose three-year-old doesn't toss his banana slices against the wall yelling swears in Spanish?

I can't help myself though. I watch them so closely.

This study tells me that I've planted bombs inside my sons that may or may not explode and destroy us all.

———

WHAT DOES IT MEAN TO HAVE A CRAZY MOM?

One February not so long ago, I sat through the worst funeral of my life. My best friend's teenaged son had wrapped himself in a cocoon of life-killing gas and gone off to sleep forever. His death was and remains the worst thing I can imagine, and I can imagine a lot.

In case you aren't sure, there is nothing worse than this death of a child, than this death of your only child, than this death of your only child by his own hand. The note he left—so kind, so like himself—I don't want you to worry about me any more, things will be better now—nearly ripped his mother in half.

His mother, my dear friend Serena (whose permission I secured to write these words), could only look to herself. What other explanation could there be? He was too young for the world to have done him in. It must have been someone something someone at home, right? Where else could the pain, the unbearable pain that killed him, have come from?

I remember her at the funeral, at the wake, in the weeks after, having to comfort other people who would come to her with their grief over her dead son.

People are, undoubtedly, the worst.

The worst thing you can say to a mother whose child just died is something like this: Being here at your kid's funeral makes me want to go home and hug my own child and appreciate him/her so much more.

That's what parents say to parents of dead kids. It's so fucking stupid. Don't ever do that.

Here's a helpful translation of your terrible words to the grieving mother: Your dead kid makes me feel really glad about my living kid.

And when the grieving mother's kid killed himself?

Translation: Your dead kid makes me feel really glad about my living kid, and I'm going to make sure that my kid never kills himself/herself like your kid did.

My friend Serena told me all of this and more, over the many beers and coffees and let's be honest, more beers, in the years since her son died. We've figured out a few things in our talks together. First, our society really doesn't know how to talk about death. Second, we really, really don't know how to talk about suicide.

It wasn't Serena's fault that her son killed himself. Of course it wasn't.

But if you can take a look into her shattered glass eyes and feel anything else but a guilt that could blow over a building then you're fit for a luncheon with Hannibal Lecter.

WHAT DOES IT MEAN TO HAVE A CRAZY MOM?

Suicide is a taboo subject. This is not news.

When I first encountered the study, I actually thought to myself, If I keep my suicide attempts secret from my sons, maybe they'll escape the curse. Like, is it knowledge of parental (whatever, mother's) suicide that causes the increased rate in children? And if I can keep that knowledge from them, would that protect them?

But now I think the reverse is true. Of course it is. I tried to die because there was no one I could tell.

Once I was healthy again, the fact of not-telling appeared before me like a magic mirror. I couldn't tell anyone I was suffering, for a variety of reasons—I was scared of involuntary committal (and losing all of the legal rights and privileges that one loses when one has been committed). I was scared my husband would leave me. I was scared my doctor would put me on medicine I didn't want to take. I was scared of people getting angry with me.

I was scared because suicide is fucking taboo.

Suicide didn't almost kill me. The taboo did. Now, when I'm feeling off, my husband can sense it—of course he can, he can sense it when I haven't had my morning coffee—and he asks me about it. What's up, babe. What do you need. I might not know the answer to that question. But he has a person on speed-dial who does.

I sit in a wooden Adirondack chair my husband made and watch my backyard sprites with their lively contrails. They zip their bikes over ramps they built. They swing from a rope swing I hung from our maple tree. They holler for me to come play pitcher for their wiffle ball game. These are my offspring. I will watch for impulsive aggression. Of course I will because I can't stop myself. But I will do more than that. I will tell them about being a proband, and about curses, and how to break them.

———

An earlier version of this chapter first appeared as an essay in *The Toast* on April 9, 2015.

1. David A. Brent, Nadine M. Melhem, Maria
Oquendo et al., "Familial Pathways to Early-Onset
Suicide Attempt: A 5.6-Year Prospective Study,"
JAMA Psychiatry, Feb. 2015, Volume 72, Issue 2,
Pages 160-168.
doi:10.1001/jamapsychiatry.2014.2141.

TRAVELING STIGMATA

I travel a lot for work. I go to conferences, give talks, do readings. My mom told me, "You should sign up for TSA Pre-Check. It'll makes things so much easier."

That seemed right. The Pre-Check lines at airport security checkpoints aren't always shorter. But at least I wouldn't have to take my shoes off or unpack my luggage in a frantic rush by the conveyor belt with some grumpy dude behind me standing in his socks.

Pre-Check, according to the TSA, is an "expedited security screening program connecting travelers departing from airports within the United States with smarter security and a better air travel experience." I didn't know much about the smarter security, but I could do without the bare feet. So who qualifies for Pre-Check? "Passengers considered low-risk who qualify for the program can receive expedited screening either as a member of the program or another specific trusted traveler group [such as active-duty military]."

After my digging around on the matter, I decided to pay a ridiculous sum of money and do a bunch of invasive paperwork to make my life a little bit easier at airports.

And in the process, I discovered more about what exactly was meant by "low-risk."

———

To get TSA Pre-Check certified, you go to this grimy yet official office—ours was located in a strip mall—where you wait in line for a while. Think the DMV, but federal. My husband and I went together, sitting side-by-side in the blue plastic chairs, waiting to give up some of our privacy and cash in exchange for convenience. The website told us what documentation to bring, and it said to set aside two hours for the process. They weren't exaggerating.

When it was my turn to step behind the curtain and be interviewed, I encountered a man with a laptop and an array of secondary devices: document scanners, fingerprint scanners, cameras, and more. He scanned my fingers. He took my picture. He scanned my many documents. It was all very *Minority Report*. Then he asked me to complete a short survey on a computer. The survey contained six total questions, the last of which was this:

6. Have you ever been found by a court or other lawful authority as lacking mental capacity or involuntarily committed to a mental institution?

In case you haven't applied for TSA Pre-Check, and in case you aren't a person with a psychiatric disability, let me explain to you what this question can do to, say, a person like me who has never been committed for her major mental illness, involuntarily or voluntarily, but who has many friends who have been. Friends who are wonderful, non-violent disabled people.

That question makes us feel like we're the scapegoats for all the evil in the world.

Think about it: Question #6, and the survey as a whole, is meant to help the TSA decide who is "safe" to allow access to an expedited route through security at airports. The TSA's job, as its name suggests, is to oversee the security of people traveling in the U.S.—and, in the extreme, this job means preventing the incomprehensible violence of events like 9/11.

This questionnaire, however, is not a scalpel; it is not strictly tailored to predicting attacks onboard airplanes. The entire Pre-Check questionnaire is instead intended to be a general pre-screening for people's propensity for violence.

———

The other queries on the questionnaire help illustrate the subtext of Question #6.

Question #1 asks about your citizenship status—only citizens and permanent residents can qualify for Pre-Check. The official reason for that policy is not one I could track down, but let's just say, like most things in the United States, Pre-Check is a privilege reserved for those with documentation.

Questions #2–5 ask about prior arrests or other involvement with the criminal justice system. The TSA, on their website, provides a long list of criminal activity that would disqualify a person from participating in Pre-Check, presumably on the grounds that past criminal activity predicts future violence—aboard airplanes, and anywhere else.

Question #6 asks whether you've ever been committed to psychiatric care—which means that, to the TSA, commitment to psychiatric care also predicts future violence.

When I got to Question #6 during my exam, I felt both a sense of dread and a sense of familiarity. The question felt familiar because, after all, I've taken the bar exam, with its intrusive and alienating mental health questions. But I also felt dread, a strange tickling on the back of my neck, that my horrible secret would get out—yes, I have a mental illness, and Question #6 reminds me that, in the eyes of my own government, this makes me abnormal—and a hair's breadth away from being considered a violent threat.

Question #6, the questions like it on the bar exam, and the questions like it on gun permit applications, tell people like me something like this: If you weren't here, there would have been no Newtown. No Navy Yard. No Columbine. All of the violent headlines would disappear with you, if you would just *go away*.

And how does that question affect normates, people who have no contact with disabled people? It confirms these irrational fears and beliefs. After all, the screening question wouldn't be there if it weren't keeping the bad guys out.

Right?

To be a scapegoat means that others place unfair blame upon you, that you take on the sins of others. Dumping blame on a scapegoat provides a small measure of peace: *If we can just keep* them *at bay, we'll be safe.*

We—people, pundits, and politicians on the left and the right—often place blame on people with psychiatric disabilities for our society's most vicious tendencies. Even politicians on the left pushed for mental health screening as a solution for gun violence. On the right, the chant is no longer just "guns don't kill people; people kill people"; it is "homicidal maniacs" kill people (to quote Wayne LaPierre of the NRA).

But LaPierre is so very wrong.

Let's take a quick look at the numbers. According to the CDC, in 2013, a total of 33,636 deaths-by-firearm occurred in the U.S. Furthermore, 84,258 people were injured by firearms. These statistics show that there is a massive amount of gun violence in the United States each year—over 117,000 injuries and deaths in 2013 alone—yet only a tiny portion of this violence can be attributed to media-magnet spree-killings perpetrated by people with mental illness. We know this, in part, because of those deaths by firearm, only a third were homicides. The rest were accidents and suicides.

Furthermore, the national media tends to ignore multiple firearm murders committed by normates, often because they are tied to "domestic violence." And domestic violence, unless it is committed by a professional athlete, isn't newsworthy.

It's true: Gun violence in our society is a large, scary, seemingly intractable problem. Over 117,000 people per year means 320 people injured or killed per day, more than 13 per hour. How do you even think about a problem that large? You can see why blaming the problem on scapegoats—people with psychiatric disabilities, or those with criminal records—might be a tidy, enticing solution, one that ameliorates some of our collective fear.

But people with psychiatric disabilities don't deserve the blame. (Nor do those with criminal records for that matter.)

The vast majority of PPDs are never violent at all, and of those who are violent, the violence is most often directed toward themselves (as the gun violence rates themselves show). Indeed, even "severe mental illness [does] not independently predict future violent behavior." Research confirms that, statistically, PPDs are no more violent than any other member of our society. However, the scientists who conduct these studies point out that convincing the public of the validity of their findings may be impossible, given the deeply ingrained fears of mental illness (see Elbogen and Johnson[1]).

In short, we, as a society, are irrationally terrified of mental illness.[2]

But what bothers me most about Question #6 is that, at its heart, it concerns medical treatment. Medical treatment should not be part of an airport survey. It's not public record. Commitment, involuntary or no, is a medical issue, not a criminal one. And we should *want* people to seek medical treatment, not scare them away by stigmatizing it.

Beyond the fact that PPDs are no more violent than any other member of society, it's important to note that people are involuntarily committed for reasons that don't necessarily correlate to their degree of psychiatric disability, and certainly not to the permanence of it. A person might have a common adverse reaction to a steroid prescribed for poison ivy or a bee sting—something called "steroid-induced psychosis." A person might have an autoimmune reaction that causes temporary psychosis. A person might be involuntarily committed because he or she is poor, a person of color, or has no family or other support system at home. (Although, let's be honest. These days, poor people, POCs, and people with no support systems are far more likely to be arrested instead.)

And in the end, the difference between involuntary commitment and voluntary commitment, so much of the time, is simply having someone tell you these words: "Just go voluntarily because otherwise you will have this on your record."

Just sign yourself in. Then you don't have to say "yes" to Question #6.

Using involuntary commitment as a proxy for potential future wrongdoing—for future violence—is not only an inaccurate metric, it is also wildly misguided. If our government, with our cultural endorsement, ties rights and privileges to the *avoidance* of medical treatment, then what we'll end up with is people who need treatment doing all they can to avoid it.

When faced with what seems like inexplicable violence, it's easy to blame a population that's either unable to or too afraid to stand up for itself. It doesn't matter what the gun violence statistics at the CDC say: It comforts people to think that perpetrators of gun violence are crazy outliers—scapegoats. But the uncomfortable truth is that this presumption is based on a lie—one that does active harm to a significant population of people.

I don't have to take my shoes off at the airport now. But every time I fly, I think about Question #6. It will always be there in the back of my mind—a reminder that I am always considered just a little suspect.

———

An earlier version of this chapter first appeared as an essay in *The Establishment* on May 12, 2016.

1. Eric B. Elbogen and Sally C. Johnson, "The Intricate Link Between Violence and Mental Disorder: Results from the National Epidemiologic Survey on Alcohol and Related Conditions," *Archives of General Psychiatry*, 2009, Volume 66, Issue 2, Pages 152-161.

2. Bruce Link et al., "Public conceptions of mental illness: labels, causes, dangerousness, and social distance," American Journal of Public Health, Sept. 1999, Volume 89, Issue 9, Pages 1328-1333.

WITH NEW LIFE COMES A FEAR OF DEATH

Before I had kids, I never worried about aging, about dying, about death. No one was counting on me, I thought, so it didn't matter if I died.

I did foolish things, before kids. Things my psychiatrist calls parasuicidal when she hears about them, when we talk about my life back then, which isn't often because mostly we talk about how hard it is to be a mom.

If you'd asked me then why I was riding a motorcycle at one hundred and twenty miles per hour, I would have told you that I had trouble feeling alive, not that I wanted to be dead. I had no intention of killing myself.

The world felt more real when I was doing dangerous things —going dangerous places in dangerous ways with dangerous people. Not because I'd been sheltered my whole life, but because I'd been numbed.

Childhood abuse will do that to you. After all, when the worst has already happened, what else is there?

No, I didn't have a death wish before I had kids. But I didn't care if I died in the pursuit of feeling something more than broken.

———

Kids, though—they break you wide open and expose parts of you that you didn't even know could feel pain. My kids have turned me into the most basic, most raw version of myself. My kids make me feel like I'm going one hundred and twenty all of the time.

It's thrilling. It's terrifying. It's exhausting.

Some days, I look at my husband, with his gentle face and mild expression, and I think, Are we living the same life together? How can he not feel it?

How can he not feel the terror in the everyday?

Perhaps my childhood did this to me, too—it enhanced everyday terrors.

I marvel that I was ever so prideful to swing my leg over a bike in the first place, knowing I might never get off again.

———

THE DAY my first son was born, I knew I was going to die.

As they rushed my premature son to the NICU and me to the operating room for an emergency procedure to try to save my life, I grabbed my husband's hand, stopping the forward movement of my stretcher. In the hospital hallway, I said to him, "You stay with him. Promise me you'll stay with him," referring to our tiny, too-early newborn son.

My husband looked so confused, the two parts of his heart, each so fragile, rolling in opposite directions.

When he didn't move to follow the baby, I released his hand. "Go with him, for me." And then I was through the double doors into the operation suite, gone from both of them, I thought, forever.

I'd done my part. I'd delivered the baby, and I'd given him to his father. Everyone was safe.

I could die, and my family would be okay.

I didn't have a death wish, and I wasn't taking risks. I didn't want to die. In fact, for the first time in my life, I was feeling the exact opposite. Even though I'd only been a mother for a few minutes, my child's life had taken hold of my psyche. Death had become terrifying.

Before the anesthesia, I started weeping. The nursed asked me what was wrong. "I won't get to hold my baby again," I said. "I wish I could have held him one more time before I died."

———

Now, I have two kids. Now, every day, I'm afraid to die.

Now, death is everywhere.

Cars are wheeled death boxes. Ladders are folding death stands. Streets are paved death zones, as opposed to the unpaved death zones, which is basically everywhere else.

The first time I had a panic attack on an airplane, I didn't know what was happening. The plane hit heavy turbulence, and, suddenly, I was struggling to breathe. Suddenly, I was weeping and shaking. I folded my body in half and clung to myself until the involuntary responses stopped.

The entire time I thought, *Who will love my children when I'm gone?*

———

LIKE MOST PARENTS, I'm also afraid for my kids.

I spent two mortgage payments on private swim lessons so that they would be safer in liquid death zones, and each child has a selection of helmets to choose from to keep him safe when using a wheeled death toy.

Every time I let them outside in the yard without my wary supervision, I run the numbers. Of all the kids on our street, on our block, in our neighborhood who play outside every day, how many come back inside, alive, well?

The odds of injury and death, it would seem, are low.

The odds do not soothe me.

———

THE SUN BENDS prismatic on the freshly-fallen snow. The kids are sledding on the hill in the alley behind our house. I'm by our neighbor's small retaining wall, taking a protective stance in case a kid heads off course. My husband stands at the bottom, where a neighbor's fence hems in the hill's run-off, ready to redirect the kids if they don't turn away soon enough.

Our sons take turns zooming down the hill, avoiding the

wall, avoiding the fence, their smiling white teeth reflecting the sun in snowy white, their joy something I could hold in my hands.

Then, our younger son veers off course. He crashes into our mailbox post. I can't move fast enough to protect him. Once at the scene, I assess, quickly. He's unhurt. I realize I've stopped breathing, and so I start again.

Earlier in the day, I pointed out the post to my husband. It's dangerous, I insisted. My husband said the mailbox was far enough away from the sledding course. "It's safe enough," he said. "Nothing to worry about."

Nothing to worry about. The odds were low.

After the crash, after I ensure my son is unhurt, I'm ready to dismantle my husband for being so careless.

"He could have died," I say.

"No," my husband says gently, "He couldn't have. Not from that. But I'll make things safer, okay?"

His loving, unspoken words: "I'll make things safer for you." And he does, building a soft barrier around the mailbox and every other potential hazard. He does these things for me, to keep the everyday terrors at bay for another afternoon.

———

An earlier version of this chapter first appeared as an essay in *Motherwell Magazine* on May 22, 2017.

ACKNOWLEDGMENTS

This book would not exist if it weren't for the magazines that first gave me the chance to write on the topics of mental health, mental illness, disability, and more—*Women in Higher Education, Chronicle Vitae, DAME Magazine, The* (late, great) *Toast*—venues where I discovered how much more honest I could be about mental health after leaving academia.

At all of these magazines, I worked with outstanding editors (many of whom have become friends), including Kera Bolonik and Jennifer Reitman at *DAME Magazine*, Liana M. Silva and Kelly J. Baker at *Women in Higher Education*, Gabriela Montell and Denise Manger at *Chronicle Vitae*, Nicole Cliffe and Nicole Chung at *The Toast*, and Liz Jackson at *Disability Stories* on Medium.

I discovered that I can't do disability writing and activism alone. My disability studies friends and my disability activist friends have blended into one group of colleagues that I rely upon daily. This list (in no particular order) is surely incomplete, and if I've forgotten you, please forgive my oversight (in fact, you should probably email me so I can add you to the next edition): Karrie Higgins, Jillian Weise, Jordynn Jack, Catherine Prendergast, Brenda Brueggemann, Margaret Price, Stephanie Kerschbaum, Zara Bain, Alice Wong, Sandra Block, Bethanne Patrick, Esme Weijun Wang, John Duffy, Jay Dolmage, and AbbyLeigh C.

Further thanks: To Lauren Faulkenberry, my dear friend, first reader, cover designer, and now business partner, for her helpful comments on this book and the exquisite cover design. To the world's best copyeditor, Janet Linger. To my Tall Poppy (tallpoppies.org) sisters for their unending support.

And thank you to my three boys, my family, always.

ABOUT THE AUTHOR

Katie Rose Guest Pryal is a novelist, journalist, essayist, and former law professor. She is the author of the Hollywood Lights novels, which include *Entanglement* and *Chasing Chaos*, and many works of nonfiction, which include her latest, *Life of the Mind Interrupted: Essays on Mental Health and Disability in Higher Education.*

As a journalist and essayist, her work has appeared in *Quartz, The Toast, Dame Magazine, The Chronicle of Higher Education,* and more. She is a member of the Tall Poppy Writers (tallpoppies.org), a group of women authors who support one another and connect with readers.

———

Stay in touch with Katie via her TinyLetter,
Writing Isn't Sexy:
tinyletter.com/krgpryal

———

A SELECTION OF KATIE'S BOOKS:

- Entanglement: A Hollywood Lights Novel
- Love & Entropy: A Hollywood Lights Novella
- Nice Wheels: A Novelette
- Chasing Chaos: A Hollywood Lights Novel
- How to Stay: A Hollywood Lights Novella
- Life of the Mind Interrupted: Essays on Mental Health and Disability in Higher Education

www.katieroseguestpryal.com